Food Guide for Soccer

Food Guide for Soccer

Tips and Recipes from the Pros

Gloria Averbuch & Nancy Clark

Photo Editor: Robyn McNeil
Cover Photo: Cori Alexander

Meyer & Meyer Sport

British Library Cataloguing in Publication Data
A catalogue record for this book is available from the British Library

Food Guide for Soccer
Maidenhead: Meyer & Meyer Sport (UK) Ltd., 2010
ISBN: 978-1-84126-288-8

© 2010 by Meyer & Meyer Sport (UK) Ltd.
Aachen, Adelaide, Auckland, Budapest, Cape Town, Graz, Indianapolis,
Maidenhead, Olten (CH), Singapore, Toronto
Member of the World
Sport Publishers' Association (WSPA)
www.w-s-p-a.org
Printed and bound by: B.O.S.S Druck und Medien GmbH, Germany
ISBN: 978-1-84126-288-8
E-Mail: info@m-m-sports.com
www.m-m-sports.com

Contents

Winning Recipes—Eating with a Purpose 161

Acknowledgements

Cori Alexander (Cover photo) and Robyn McNeil (Photo Editor), two wonderful photographers; Women's Professional Soccer (WPS); Rob Penner, Director of Communications, WPS; Doron Tamari, for research and invaluable player interviews; Thomas Hofstetter and Gerry Marrone, my leaders at Sky Blue FC; Nancy's and Gloria's family for being patient recipe testers.

Dedication

My Journey with Women's Professional Soccer

When my 23-year-old daughter, Yael, was in the fifth grade, her teacher asked each student to stand and tell the class the job to which they aspired.
"Professional soccer player," Yael said with pride.
"No," the teacher replied, somewhat annoyed, "Name a real profession."
While I had all but forgotten this incident, it was the first story Yael told after she was drafted to Sky Blue FC of the new Women's Professional Soccer (WPS) league. She had nurtured her dream, without doubt or deviation, and now, she wondered how that teacher would react to know it had come true.

For weeks after the first pre-season training began, Yael would say she had to pinch herself every day, because she couldn't believe the game she so loved could be called "a job."

Her opportunities, and the chance to live a dream, inspire in me the same feeling I get when I watch her sister, Shira, play at Stanford—with a team and a university my youngest daughter has come to love.

Yael's dream, and her joy, is mirrored all over the league. Those of us involved experience it when we watch the players, and we can see it on the faces of the young girls, the families, the fans, and the people who work in Women's Professional Soccer.

I am gratified to have worked for Sky Blue FC and Women's Professional Soccer since its inception. I recall the thrill of casting our team's vote on the league name and logo, and seeing the results of our efforts in the capacity crowd at our first-ever home game, and more, as the team hoisted the first-ever league Championship trophy.

When people ask me about the greatest benefit of working in sports and soccer, and watching my children, and others' children, play this game, I answer that to nurture and possess a passion is a gift given to the most fortunate among us. For millions, both here and around the world, soccer is the vehicle for that passion.

I dedicate this book to all those who are passionate, especially among them Women's Professional Soccer Commissioner Tonya Antonucci, who too had a dream, and didn't let go of it, and to all the players and soccer families with whom I have been privileged to 'break bread'—and in so doing, create a community of which I am proud to be a part.

And finally, to Christie Rampone and Mike Lyons, two amazing coaches and human beings, who took Sky Blue FC from nowhere to win the 2009 inaugural Women's Professional Soccer Championship.

Gloria Averbuch

To all aspiring soccer stars—eat wisely and well, and win with good nutrition!

Nancy Clark

Foreword

The Soccer Nutrition Connection

My light bulb moment happened in the summer of 1997, as a parent on a New Jersey summer select Under-10 girls soccer team, the Stampede. While the girls triumphed in the morning tournament games, their performance regularly slipped in the late afternoon games. "I guess we're just not an afternoon team," the coach lamented. Having had a background in sports, fitness and nutrition, including contributing to a previous book with my co-author and sports nutritionist Nancy Clark, I suddenly thought, "Wait a minute; there is no such thing as a 'morning' or an 'afternoon' team!"

"Money!" I yelled. I needed cash in my race to find a supermarket in a strange town. I literally sped through the aisles, grabbing bananas, bottles of sports drinks, yogurt cups and other high-energy snacks, then rushed back in time for the team to consume and digest these goodies before the next game.

That afternoon, the Stampede triumphed. Thus began a season in which the players, families and coaches became immersed in sports nutrition education and how to fuel with a purpose (to win!). Over two summers, the Stampede amassed an astounding record of 55 wins, 5 losses, and 5 ties. Did nutrition make the difference?

Perhaps the answer is in one 2-0 loss, when the team was forced to play without the accustomed pre-game group fueling. Two weeks later, fueled on their pre-game "power snacks," they beat the same team 2-1. But more importantly, over time they developed a sense of pride, empowerment and camaraderie that they were taking control, and doing their best to be successful. And that success eventually translated to life both on and off the field.

Shortly after that first weekend, I made a call to Nancy. She worked with me to develop an eating plan that impacted this team (many are still playing at age 22), and the multitude of teams of all ages I have been involved with ever since. Over time, these teams have taken the information Nancy and I shared, and gone on to become winners.

What is "winning" however? Yes, it is reflected on the scoreboard, but that first season, it was also evident in the 10-year-old who spontaneously vowed, "I'm never going to drink soda again!" She associated that scoreboard with good nutrition, and her lesson—one that came from her direct experience, was a powerful illustration of true personal victory.

Together with other parents and coaches, I have continued to instill positive sports nutrition habits and team rituals through a decade of youth teams, and even onto the college level, at the fabled University of North Carolina, where my older daughter, Yael, was on two NCAA National Championship teams. Even the most famous, the winningest team in Division 1 college sports, has benefited from adopting new eating rituals.

And now, with the support of Women's Professional Soccer, considered by most to be the highest-level women's soccer league in the world, Nancy and I fulfill a desire we have discussed for many years to get valuable sports nutrition information between covers in this book by bringing these same wonderful principles to the soccer community and the fans of Women's Professional Soccer.

You are about to embark on one of the most wonderful aspects of your, or your child's, soccer career. Understanding the principles of good sports nutrition (which is also good nutrition for life), it is completely reasonable to expect a player and team to discover a whole new level of play, and of excellence. It is an opportunity to add resistance to injury, enhanced recovery between games, and just as important, a lifetime of good eating habits. It is an opportunity for a conscientious parent, coach or teammate to make a significant impact on their players' lives.

So, let soccer be your teacher. Enjoy yet another aspect of "the beautiful game," — the chance to foster good health, pleasurable eating, and success in life—both on and off the field.

Gloria Averbuch and Nancy Clark

Preface

To all the soccer players, soccer parents, soccer coaches and soccer fans out there, it has been a pleasure to launch the first season of Women's Professional Soccer in 2009. The league has laid the first cornerstones and built a solid foundation to develop a long-lasting and sustainable future for a professional women's league in this country.

Most importantly, the first year of WPS showcased an incredible level of international soccer talent and a world class product out on the field. Games were exciting and close, goals were frequently scored in bunches, and stadiums provided the very family-friendly atmospheres and affordable fun for which we all strived.

The players in Women's Professional Soccer are the league's biggest asset. They are incredible athletes, exceptional role models and dedicated teammates all in one; some are even mothers, coaches or hold other leadership positions.

All of us who are passionate about soccer know how it becomes part of the entire household—from weekday practices to weekend tournaments; from morning discussions of the latest soccer news to evening mealtime, when soccer players fuel up on dinner after a hard practice.

Nutrition is an important part of any elite athlete's daily routine, and we are glad that the players of Women's Professional Soccer have shared their fueling tips, food ideas, favorite recipes and thoughtful nutrition suggestions with the authors of this book. We all know that everyone will always win with good nutrition!

We hope to see you all at a WPS game in the near future. Otherwise, catch your favorite players on TV or follow them online at the WPS league website. You can learn a lot from the pros just by watching.

Tonya Antonucci
WPS Commissioner

About Women's Professional Soccer (WPS)

Women's Professional Soccer (WPS) is the premier women's soccer league in the world and the global standard by which women's professional sports are measured. The inaugural season kicked off in 2009, with WPS teams based in the Bay Area, Boston, Chicago, Los Angeles, New Jersey/New York, St. Louis, and Washington, D.C. The league's eighth and ninth franchises, Philadelphia and Atlanta, began play in 2010.

SECTION I
DAY-TO-DAY EATING FOR ENERGY

Chapter 1
Daily Eating for Health and High Energy

Eating with a purpose, and also with enjoyment—that's what nutrition for soccer is all about! Good food is not only one of life's pleasures; it is also a powerful tool for helping you to be a better soccer player. Eating the right foods at the right times can help you train at your best so you can then compete at your best. It will also improve your health and future well-being. Unfortunately, eating well on a daily basis doesn't just happen magically. You need to understand good nutrition, and find time to food shop, so you'll have wholesome sports foods available. You also need to find time to fuel up and refuel with an eating schedule that enhances your energy and improves your performance. Unfortunately, the chaos of training and general schedules that lead to erratic eating patterns may result in losing track of what you have—and have not—eaten.

In this chapter, you will learn the basic tips about how to eat well, even when you are eating on the run. But first, it helps to understand what "eating well" means. A simple definition is to eat:

Some Top Sports Foods

The following top sports foods offer mainly cook-free and convenient best bets for soccer players (and their families) who eat and run.

Some of the best fruits for vitamins A and/or C or potassium: oranges, grapefruit, cantaloupe, bananas, apricots, strawberries, kiwi, mango

Some of the best vegetables for vitamins A and/or C: broccoli, spinach, green and red peppers, tomatoes, carrots, sweet potato, winter squash

The easiest sources of calcium for strong bones: Low-fat milk, yogurt, cheese, calcium-fortified orange juice, soy milk, and tofu

Convenient cook-free proteins for building and protecting muscles: Deli roast beef, ham, and turkey, canned tuna and salmon, hummus, peanut butter, tofu, cottage cheese

Cook-free grains for carbohydrates and fiber: High-fiber breakfast cereals (preferably iron-enriched), wholesome breads and bagels, whole-grain crackers

1. At least three kinds of wholesome foods at each meal.

2. At least two kinds of wholesome foods for each snack.

3. Evenly-sized meals about every four hours throughout the day (as opposed to "crescendo eating" with a small breakfast and a large meal at the end of the day).

4. At least 90% of the calories from quality foods and, if desired, the remaining 10% from sweets and treats.

Luckily for today's soccer players, you (or your parents) don't have to be a good cook to eat well. You can still manage to nourish your body optimally even if you are dashing from school or work to workout, and are spending very little time in the kitchen.

Here are some guidelines to help you make optimal food choices:

• Try to eat at least 2 cups of fruit and $2^{1}/_{2}$ cups of vegetables per day.

• Choose a variety of colors of fruits and vegetables each day: red apples, green peppers, orange carrots, yams, or white potatoes. If you can't eat them, drink fruit and/or vegetable juices.

- Enjoy whole-grain products at least two times per day, such as oatmeal for breakfast and whole wheat bread for lunch. The rest of the recommended grains can come from enriched grain products, such as enriched pasta. In general, at least half the grains should come from whole grains. (Whole grains include whole wheat, brown rice, oats, corn, barley, etc.)

- Drink 3 cups (24 ounces; 720 ml) each day of fat-free or low-fat (soy) milk or yogurt, or eat the calcium-equivalent in low-fat cheese (1.5 ounces (45 g) of cheese = 8 ounces (240 ml) of milk or yogurt).

- When selecting and preparing meat, poultry, dry beans, and milk or milk products, make choices that are lean, low-fat, or fat-free.

Dietary Recommendations for Good Health

By following these dietary recommendations, you can substantially reduce your risk of developing heart disease and other diseases of aging. If you are a growing athlete, the guidelines can help you create good eating habits for both sports and life.

- Balance calorie intake and physical activity to achieve and maintain a healthy body weight.
- Consume a diet rich in vegetables and fruits.
- Choose whole-grain, high-fiber foods.
- Consume fish, especially oily fish, at least twice a week.
- Limit your intake of saturated fat to $<7\%$ of energy, trans fat to $<1\%$ of energy, and cholesterol to <300 mg per day by:
  — choosing lean meats and vegetable alternatives.
  — selecting fat-free (skim), 1 %-fat, and low-fat dairy products.
  — minimizing intake of partially hydrogenated fats.
- Minimize your intake of beverages and foods with added sugars.
- When you eat food that is prepared outside of the home, follow these dietary recommendations.

Source: Diet and Lifestyle Recommendation Revision 2006: A Scientific Statement From the American Heart Association Nutrition Committee. A. Lichtenstein et al. *Circulation* 2006; 114:82-96.

- Limit your intake of saturated and trans fats and choose healthier oils such as olive and canola oils, nuts and nut butters, and oily fish such as salmon.

Many soccer players and their families wonder about eating organic. While that answer is complex, we simply recommend you choose in-season, locally grown foods whenever possible. Go organic if you wish, but first and foremost, remember that the priority is to get the basics right. That means your soccer diet (or that of your children), should not be a random affair, or routinely a fast food stop. Be responsible, plan ahead and take meal times seriously.

Balancing Your Diet

Food can be divided into four groups: grain, fruit & vegetable, dairy, and protein. The trick to balancing the recommended servings of foods during your day is to plan to have at least three out of four food groups per meal, and one or two food groups per snack, such as:

		Breakfast	Lunch	Snack	Dinner	Snack
1.	Grain	bran flakes	bread		spaghetti	popcorn
2.	Fruit & Vegetable	banana	apple baby carrots	berries	tomato sauce	cider
3.	Dairy	milk		yogurt	Parmesan cheese	
4.	Protein	almonds	tuna fish		ground turkey	

"When I eat as healthy as possible, I feel better overall, and in the long run perform better. My body is more resilient; I have rarely been sick since I started eating well-balanced meals throughout the day."

Nicole Barnhart, Goalkeeper, FC Gold Pride

Eat Right for Yourself, And for Your Team

Just as each teammate depends on the others to be fit, focused and ready to play, so too with being well-nourished. When you eat right, you do so for yourself and for the team effort, since what, when and how you fuel has a direct impact on your performance. Parents, coaches, team captains and/or managers: take a poll before games. Ask players what and when they ate before arriving. If it isn't up to speed (often that means not enough), pass the pre-game snacks. Gloria's teams made sure to do this, particularly for important games. The players soon got the message, and learned to eat well on their own.

Carbohydrates for Your Sports Diet

By eating grains, fruits and vegetables as the foundation of each meal, you'll consume about 55 to 65% of your calories from carbohydrates. This is exactly what you need for a high-energy sports diet. These carbohydrates are stored in muscles in the form of glycogen and provide the energy you need for performing on the soccer field.

Grain foods are a popular source of carbohydrates for most soccer athletes. The exceptions are the weight-conscious athletes who believe they will get fat if they eat breads, cereals and pastas at each meal. False. Carbohydrates are not fattening; excess calories are fattening. (See Chapter 14 for an explanation of calorie needs.)

"When I eat carbs, I try to make them healthy choices, like whole-wheat pasta and bread."

Tina Ellertson, Defender, Saint Louis Athletica

Fruits and vegetables are also excellent sources of carbohydrates. But some players have trouble figuring out how to consume the recommended daily 2 cups (500 g) of fruits and $2^1/_2$ cups (600 g) of vegetables. As one 22-year-old sheepishly remarked, "I'm lucky if I eat that much in a week." The trick is to eat large portions. Most soccer players can easily enjoy a banana (counts as one cup fruit) and 8 ounces (one cup) of orange juice in the morning. That's already the minimal 2 cups of fruit for the day! A big bowl of salad filled with colorful tomato, carrot, and pepper can account for the minimal recommended $2^1/_2$ cups of vegetables.

Fruits: Recommended Daily Intake—2 or more cups (500+ g)

Here's what counts as "one cup"; hungry soccer players can easily consume double portions and achieve the recommended intake of two or more cups per day.

Orange Juice	8 ounces	240 ml
Apple	1 small	100 g
Banana	1 small	100 g
Canned Fruit	1 cup	240 g
Dried fruit	$^1/_2$ cup	80 g

Vegetables: Recommended Daily Intake—$2^1/_2$ to 3+ cups (600 to 700+ g)

Here's what counts as "one cup"; plan to eat double!

Broccoli	1 medium stalk	200 g
Spinach	2 cups raw	60 g
Salad Bar	1 average bowl	100 g
Spaghetti Sauce (Tomato)	1 cup	250 g

Fruits and vegetables are truly nature's vitamin pills, chock full of vitamin C (to help with healing), beta-carotene (to protect against cancer), fiber (to aid with regular bowel movements), and numerous other vitamins and minerals. The sidebar, *Eat More Veggies!* offers suggestions for ways to boost your veggie intake simply.

Eat More Veggies!

If you struggle to consume the recommended two to three servings of vegetables per day, the following tips may help you to enhance your vegetable intake — and your health.

- Eat more of the best vegetables, less of the rest. In general, colorful dark green, deep yellow, orange, and red vegetables have far more nutrients than pale ones. Hence, if you dislike pale zucchini, summer squash, and cucumbers, don't work hard to acquire a taste for them. Instead, put your efforts into having more broccoli, spinach, and winter squash — the richly colored, more nutrient-dense choices.

- Include lettuce, tomato and green or red peppers on your sandwiches and wraps.

- Keep baby carrots and cherry tomatoes handy in the front of the refrigerator for easy snacking.

- Bring a baggie of cut up veggies to practices, games, and tournaments. In an environment with hungry, thirsty young players, you'll be surprised how popular veggies are, and how quickly they get eaten — particularly if you include a low-fat ranch dressing for a dip!

- Eat colorful salads filled with tomatoes, green peppers, carrots, spinach, and dark lettuces. Pale salads with white lettuce, cucumbers, onions, celery, and other pale veggies offer little more than crunch. When smothered with dressing, this crunch becomes highly caloric. Alternatives to a pale restaurant salad include tomato juice, vegetable soup, a steamed veggie or, when you get home, a handful of raw baby carrots for a bedtime snack.

- Fortify spaghetti sauce with a box of frozen chopped broccoli or green peppers. Cook the veggies alongside the spaghetti (in a steamer over the pasta water) before you add them to the tomato sauce.

- Choose fast foods with the most veggies:

  — Pizza with peppers, mushrooms and extra tomato sauce
  — Chinese entrées stir-fried with vegetables
  — Lunchtime V-8 juice instead of diet soda

- Even over-cooked vegetables are better than no vegetables. If your only option is over-cooked veggies from the cafeteria, eat them. While cooking does destroy some of the vegetable's nutrients, it does not destroy all of them. Any vegetable is better than no vegetable!

- Keep frozen vegetables stocked in your freezer, ready and waiting. They are quick and easy to prepare, won't spoil quickly, and have more nutrients than "fresh" vegetables that have been in the store and your refrigerator for a few days. Because cooking (more than freezing) reduces a vegetable's nutritional content:

  — Quickly cook vegetables only until tender crisp and use the cooking water as a broth.
  — Microwave vegetables in a covered dish.
  — Stir-fry them with very little olive oil.

- Use a blender to finely chop veggies to include in meatloaf, soup, and stews.

- When all else fails, eat fruit to help compensate for lack of vegetables. The best alternatives include bananas, oranges, grapefruit, melon, strawberries, blueberries and kiwi. These choices are rich in many of the same nutrients found in vegetables.

For more information on serving sizes and ways to add more vegetables to your daily diet, see: www.MyPyramid.gov

Protein for Your Sports Diet

Like carbohydrates, protein-rich foods are also an important part of your sports diet. You should eat a protein-rich food at each meal. Some soccer players tend to either *over-* or *under-* consume protein, depending on their ideas about healthy eating and lifestyle. While it is true that young athletes have an increased need for protein due to the demands of their sports and the fact they are growing, most tend to consume more than they require.

Whereas high-protein eaters may frequently choose cheese omelets, fast food burgers and other meals filled with saturated fats, others bypass these foods in their efforts to eat a low-fat or vegetarian diet—but they neglect to replace beef with beans, or other appropriate substitutes. Or they equate healthy eating with low-cal protein like skinless chicken breast and avoid important carbs and good fats. (For additional information and guidelines on how to choose the best balance of protein, see Chapter 6.)

Recommended daily protein intake:
5 to 7 ounces (or ounce-equivalents; 140 to 200 g)

Protein-rich Foods	Soccer Player's Portion	Number of ounces or ounce-equivalents
Tuna	6 oz (170 g) can, drained	3-4
Chicken	6-ounce breast	6
Peanut Butter	2-4 tablespoons	1-2
Kidney Beans	1 cup	2

To meet your protein requirement, you should consume not only one or two protein-rich foods per day, but also the recommended 2 to 3 servings of calcium-rich dairy foods such as milk, yogurt and cheese (or calcium-fortified soy milk). Calcium is particularly important for growing teens and women who should optimize bone density. For only 300 calories, soccer players can easily achieve the recommended calcium intake—plus boost their protein intake—by consuming:
• 8 oz (240 ml) of milk or soy milk on breakfast cereal
• 8 oz (240 ml) tub of yogurt with lunch
• a (decaf) latte made with skim or low-fat milk for an afternoon energizer

When choosing the recommended 2 to 3 daily servings of dairy foods, note that fat-free and low-fat products are preferable for heart-health and calorie control, but you need not suffer with "watery" skim milk if you really don't like it. You can try the new thicker forms of skim milk on the market. Or, you can always cut back on fat in other parts of your diet. For example, Patty, a midfielder on a collegiate soccer team, opted for cereal with reduced-fat (2%) milk (5 grams of fat per cup), but saved on fat elsewhere in her diet by using fat-free salad dressing and eating low-fat granola. (For more information on dietary fat, see Chapter 7.)

Soccer athletes who prefer a dairy-free diet or are lactose intolerant should take special care to eat adequate amounts of nondairy calcium sources. See the sidebar, *Calcium Equivalents* for food suggestions.

Calcium Equivalents

The recommended daily calcium intake is:

Age Group	Calcium (mg)
Teens, 9-18 years	1,300
Adults, 19-50 years	1,000
Adults, 51+ years	1,200-1,500

The following foods all provide about 300 milligrams of calcium. Three choices per day, or one at each meal, will contribute to meeting your calcium needs.

	Calcium-rich Foods	Amount for 300 mg calcium	
Dairy	milk, whole or skim	1 cup	(240 ml)
	yogurt	1 cup	(230 g)
	cheese	1$\frac{1}{2}$ ounces	(45 g)
	cottage cheese	2 cups	(450 g)
	frozen yogurt	1$\frac{1}{2}$ cups	(150 g)
Proteins	soy milk	1 cup	(240 ml)
	tofu	8 ounces	(250 g)
	salmon, canned with bones	5 ounces	(140 g)
	sardines, canned with bones	3 ounces	(85 g)
	almonds	4 ounces	(110 g)
Vegetables	broccoli, cooked	3 cups	(550 g)
	collard or turnip greens, cooked	1 cup	(150 g)
	kale or mustard greens, cooked	1$\frac{1}{2}$ cups	(220 g)

Many female athletes tend to consume a shockingly low amount of calcium. While we don't recommend supplements in place of food, if you don't consume a calcium-rich dairy food or a calcium fortified food with each meal (such as fortified orange juice or soy milk), taking supplemental calcium, in combination with Vitamin D, is a smart idea.

Sweets and Treats

Although nutritionists recommend eating a wholesome diet based on grains, fruits, and vegetables, some soccer athletes eat a diet with too many sweets and treats. If you have a junk-food diet, you may be able to correct this imbalance by eating more wholesome foods *before you get too hungry*. Athletes who get too hungry (or who avoid carbohydrates) tend to choose sugary, fatty foods (such as apple pie, instead of apples). A simple solution to the junk-food diet is to prevent hunger by eating heartier portions of wholesome foods at meals. And once you replace sweets with more wholesome choices (including whole grain carbs), your craving for sweets will diminish.

Take note: You need not eat a "perfect diet" (*no* fats, *no* sugar) to have a good diet. Nothing is nutritionally wrong with having something sweet, such as a cookie, for dessert after having eaten a sandwich, milk, and fruit for lunch. But a lot is wrong with eating cookies for lunch and skipping the sandwich. That's when both nutrition and performance problems arise.

The key to balancing fats and sugars appropriately in your diet is to abide the following guidelines:

* 10% of your calories can appropriately come from refined sugar. (about 200-300 calories from sugar per day for most soccer players)
* 25% of your calories can appropriately come from (preferably healthful) fat. (about 450-750 calories from fat per day, or roughly 50-85 grams of fat per day)

Hence, moderate amounts of chips, cookies, and ice cream can fit into an overall healthful food plan, if desired.

Need Some Help Shaping Up Your Diet?

If you want personalized dietary advice, Nancy recommends you seek professional advice from a registered dietitian (RD) who specializes in sports nutrition and, ideally, is Board Certified as a Specialist in Sports Dietetics (CSSD). To find a sports nutritionist in your area, use the referral networks at the American Dietetic Association's website (www.eatright.org) or the website of

ADA's practice group of sports dietitians (www.SCANdpg.org). Or try googling "sports nutritionist, your city." You'll be glad you did! This personal nutrition coach can help you win with good nutrition. Better yet, consider doing this on a teamwide basis, and get group nutrition analysis and education.

Summary

Nutrition for soccer is all about eating with a purpose so you can then enjoy the benefits of high energy and good health. Your food goals are to eat at least three kinds of wholesome foods at each meal; at least two kinds of wholesome foods for each snack; evenly-sized meals about every four hours throughout the day (as opposed to "crescendo eating" with a small breakfast and a large meal at the end of the day); at least 90% of the calories from quality foods and, if desired, the remaining 10% from sweets and treats. You need not eat a "perfect diet" to have a good diet, but you do want to choose more of the best foods (wholesome grains, fruits, vegetables, low-fat dairy, and lean meats or beans) and less of the rest.

Chapter 2
Breakfast: The Meal of Champions

If you want to "get it right" in terms of establishing a good sports diet that helps make you a better soccer player, there's no doubt breakfast is *the* most important meal of the day. Yes, there can be hurdles to eating breakfast, but the benefits far outweigh the difficulties. Breakfast eaters tend to:

- eat a more nutritious, lower fat diet.
- have lower blood cholesterol levels.
- enjoy success with weight control.
- are mentally alert and more productive—in school and on the field.
- have more energy to enjoy exercise either in the morning or later in the day.

As an aspiring soccer star, plan to start your day with breakfast preferably within two hours of waking. From female athletes on a 1,800-calorie weight reduction diet, to tall men who devour 3,600 calories a day, soccer athletes deserve to eat a hefty 500 to 900 calories for their morning meal(s). If you train in the morning (such as in summer camps or team pre-season), you might want to eat part of your breakfast (as tolerated) before practice, and then enjoy the rest of the breakfast afterwards, either at home, on the way to class, or in your car. (See Chapter 13 for information on how to calculate your calorie needs for breakfast and the entire day.)

Despite our clear message about breakfast being the most important meal of the day, we have to coax many soccer athletes to experiment with eating (more) breakfast. Far too many of them under-eat in the morning. Let's take at look at some standard breakfast excuses—and solutions.

I don't have time: Lack of *priority* is the real problem, not lack of time. If you can make time to train, you can make time to fuel for your training. Even if you choose to sleep to the last minute before dragging yourself out of bed to go to school, work, or a soccer practice or game, you can still choose to eat breakfast on the way. Some simple portable breakfasts include:

- a baggie filled with raisins, almonds, and granola.
- a tortilla rolled with a slice or two of low-fat cheese.
- a peanut butter and honey sandwich on wholesome bread.
- a glass of milk, then a banana while on the way to your destination.
- a travel mug filled with a fruit smoothie or protein shake.
- an energy bar and a banana during the morning commute.

The key to a grab-'n'-go breakfast is to *plan ahead*. Prepare your breakfast the night before. For example, on the weekends, you might want to make the Carrot Apple Muffins on page 167 or buy a dozen bagels. Pre-slice the bread or the bagels, wrap the desired portion in individual plastic bags, and put them in the freezer. Take one out of the freezer at night so breakfast will be ready and waiting in the morning, or give it a few seconds straight from the freezer into the microwave.

MORE GRAB & GO BREAKFAST IDEAS

You can make pancakes or French toast (preferably whole grain) ahead of time and freeze. Or prepare it fresh and ready to eat on the road. Make a "pancake sandwich" with peanut or other nut better and jelly. Add bananas or other fruit, baked into the pancakes or as an addition to the sandwich.

Cereal Sandwiches—This pre-game ritual of a top soccer player brought a lot of laughs, but then caught on with her team: spread peanut or other nut butter on bread, and sprinkle on dry cereal—such as Fiber One, Bran Flakes, Grape-Nuts, etc. Makes a crunchy 2-in-1 breakfast!

Breakfast interferes with my training schedule: If you have an early soccer practice or game (8:00 to 10:00 A.M.), you will likely play better and avoid an energy crash if you eat at least part of your breakfast beforehand. (You might have to slowly train your stomach to tolerate this fuel). A swig of juice, a chunk of bagel, or piece of bread are popular choices that can at least get your blood sugar on the upswing, contribute to greater stamina, and help you feel more awake. If you just cannot tolerate this food, a hefty bedtime snack the night before can reduce the risk of a morning energy lag. (Chapter 10 explains in greater detail the importance of morning food.)

Breakfast is equally important if you train or compete at mid-day or in the afternoon. You need to fuel up early in order to frontload your energy for quality training or competing later in the day.

"I used to eat plain oatmeal for breakfast, but I found myself getting hungry at the end of a long practice. I started adding sliced raw almonds for protein and fat, and now I stay satisfied longer."

Rachel Buehler, Defender, FC Gold Pride

I'm not hungry in the morning: If you have no morning appetite, chances are you ate your breakfast calories the night before. Perhaps you ate a huge dinner? Big bowl of ice cream? Too many cookies before bedtime? The solution to having no morning appetite, obviously, is to eat less at night so that you can start the day off hungry. Eating breakfast should become a habit; reverse your eating pattern and get used to eating in the morning!

If playing soccer first thing in the morning "kills your appetite" (due to the rise in body temperature), keep in mind that you *will* be hungry within a brief time afterwards when you have cooled down. Plan ahead, so when the "hungry horrors" hit, you will have healthful options ready and waiting.

I'm on a diet: Too many weight-conscious soccer players start their diets at breakfast. Bad idea. Breakfast skippers tend to gain weight and to be heavier than breakfast eaters. A satisfying breakfast *prevents you from getting too hungry* and overeating later in the day.

Your best bet for successful dieting is to eat *during the day*, burn off the calories, and then eat a lighter meal at night. (Chapter 14 has more details about how to lose weight and still have energy to train.)

Breakfast makes me hungrier: Many soccer players complain that if they eat breakfast, they seem to get hungrier and eat more all day. This may result from thinking they have already "blown their diets" by eating breakfast, so they might as well keep overeating, then start dieting again the next day. Wrong. Successful diets start at breakfast.

If you feel hungry after breakfast you probably ate *too little* breakfast. For example, 100 calories of toast with jam is enough to whet your appetite but not to satisfy your calorie needs. Try budgeting about one-quarter of your daily calories for breakfast—500-600 calories for most 120-150 pound players. This translates into two slices of toast with jam, a banana, low-fat yogurt, and juice; or yogurt and a bagel.

Note: If you overeat at breakfast, you can easily resolve the problem by eating less at lunch or dinner. You won't be as physically hungry for those meals and will easily be able to eat smaller portions.

The Breakfast of Champions

By now, we hope we've convinced you that breakfast is indeed the most important meal of the day. *What* is a good choice to eat, you wonder?

Nancy highly recommends cereal. Cereal is quick, convenient, and filled with the calcium, iron, carbohydrates, fiber, and other nutrients soccer players need. A bowl of whole grain cereal with fruit and low-fat milk provides a well-balanced meal that includes three of the four food groups (grain, milk, and fruit) and sets the stage for an overall low-fat diet.

Cereal is versatile. Mix brands and vary the flavor with different toppings:
* sliced banana
* blueberries (a handful of frozen ones also tastes great—especially if microwaved)
* raisins
* canned fruit
* cinnamon
* maple syrup
* vanilla yogurt

Nancy's personal favorite is to put a mix of cereals in a bowl, top it with fresh, frozen or canned fruit (depending on the season), heat it in the microwave for 30 to 60 seconds, and then add cold milk. It's like eating fruit cobbler! Women's Professional Soccer players have all kinds of combo favorites as well, such as raw oats with crunchy Grape Nuts or Fiber One, adding chopped fresh or dried fruit, cinnamon and a little vanilla extract. Why not try the FC Gold Pride Good Grain Granola in the Recipe Section, page 168!

Nontraditional Breakfasts

Not everyone likes cereal for breakfast, nor do they want to cook eggs or pancakes. If what to eat for breakfast stumps you, choose a food that you enjoy. After all, you'll be more likely to eat breakfast if it tastes good. Remember that any food — even a cookie (preferably oatmeal raisin, rather than chocolate chip) — is better than nothing.

How about:
* leftover pizza
* leftover Chinese, Mexican or other dinner food
* mug of tomato soup
* potato (or sweet potato/yam) zapped in the microwave while you take your shower
* tuna sandwich
* peanut butter and apple
* protein bar

"I like to eat granola and fruit for breakfast before a game, and then I wear my lucky sports bra."

Heather Mitts, Defender, Philadelphia Independence

How to Choose the Best Breakfast Cereal

Needless to say, all cereals are not created equal. By reading the Nutrition Facts on the cereal box, you can see that some offer more nutritional value than others. Also keep in mind that hungry soccer athletes generally need more than one serving (a standard unit of measure) of cereal; they need a larger portion (the amount chosen to satisfy the appetite) that contributes additional nutrients.

Here are four tips to help you make the best cereal choices.

1. **Choose iron-enriched cereals with at least 25% of the Daily Value for iron to help prevent anemia.**
   Note, however, the iron in breakfast cereals is poorly absorbed compared to the iron in lean red meats. But you can enhance iron absorption by drinking a glass of orange juice or enjoying another source of vitamin C (such as grapefruit, cantaloupe, strawberries, or kiwi) along with the cereal. And *any* iron is better than no iron.
   If you tend to eat "all-natural" types of cereals, such as some granolas and shredded wheat, be aware that these types have "no additives," hence no added iron. You might want to mix and match all-natural brands with iron-enriched brands (or make the effort to eat iron-rich foods at other meals).

2. **Choose fiber-rich (such as bran) cereals with more than 5 grams of fiber per serving.**
   Fiber not only helps prevent constipation, but is also a protective nutrient that may reduce your risk of colon cancer and heart disease. Whole grain and bran cereals are the best sources of fiber, more so than even fruits and vegetables. Choose from All-Bran, Raisin Bran, Bran Chex, Fiber One, or any of the numerous cereals with "bran" or "fiber" in the name. You can also mix high- and low-fiber cereals (Rice Crispies + Fiber One; Special K + Raisin Bran) to boost their fiber value. Fiber-rich cereal is good for soccer

players also because it is a more sustained energy source than refined grains, and thus fuels you for the long run.

Note: If you have trouble with diarrhea when training, you may want to forgo bran cereals! The extra fiber may aggravate the situation.

3. **Choose cereals with whole grains listed among the first ingredients.**
Whole grains include whole wheat, brown rice, and oats; these should be listed first in the ingredients. Nancy suggests you pay more attention to a cereal's grain content than its sugar or sodium (salt) content. Sugar is a simple carbohydrate that fuels your muscles. Yes, sugar calories are nutritionally empty calories. But when they are combined with milk, banana, and the cereal itself, the twenty empty calories in 5 grams of added sugar are insignificant. Obviously, sugar-filled frosted flakes and kids' cereals with 15 grams of sugar or more per serving are somewhat more like dessert than breakfast. Hence, try to limit your breakfast choices to cereals with fewer than 5 grams of added sugar per serving. Enjoy the sugary ones for snacks or dessert, if desired, or mix a little with low-sugar cereals.

4. **Choose primarily low-fat cereals with less than 2 grams of fat per serving.**
High-fat cereals such as some brands of granola and crunchy cookie-type cereals can add unexpected fat and calories to your sports diet. Select low-fat brands for the foundation of your breakfast; then use only a sprinkling of the higher-fat treats, if desired, for a topping.

Mix 'n Match Cereals

When it comes to cereals, you may not find one that meets all of your standards for high fiber, high iron and low fat, but you can always mix-and-match to create a winning combination. The list below highlights how different cereals offer different benefits. Check the nutritional labels of your favorites as well.

Cereal is not for breakfast only! We encourage our players to fill a baggie with cereal to take to games for a convenient post-competition snack. Another fun idea is to "crunch up" other foods and add nutrition with cereal toppings—such as on oatmeal, in yogurt or even in sandwiches.

Brand		Iron (%DV)	Fiber (g)	Fat (g)
The "Ideal cereal"		>25%	>5	<2
Cheerios, 1 cup	(30g)	45%	3	2
Wheaties, 1 cup	(30 g)	45%	3	1
Kashi Go Lean, 1 cup	(52 g)	10%	10	1
Raisin Bran, Kellogg's 1 cup	(59 g)	25%	7	1.5
Fiber One, $1/_2$ cup	(30 g)	25%	14	1
Quaker 100% Natural, $1/_2$ cup	(48 g)	6%	3	6
Oat Squares, Quaker, 1 cup	(60 g)	80%	4	2.5
Cap'n Crunch, $3/_4$ cup	(30 g)	25%	1	1.5

Breakfast on the Road

At a restaurant, you can be confronted with fat-laden cheese omelets, hash browns, sausage, and buttery toast. Take the higher carb route by ordering a fruit cup, oatmeal, and/or egg whites and whole-wheat bagel with jam. If you want a bigger breakfast, or if you've played a hard game, refuel with pancakes (increasingly available in whole wheat) or French toast. Order a large orange juice or tomato juice to help compensate for a potential lack of fruits or veggies in the other meals.

What about Coffee?

Some soccer players jump out of bed, ready to jump into a busy day. Others search for a morning cup of coffee or other caffeinated beverage to help start their engines. (Caffeine is a proven energy enhancer, which is further discussed in Chapter 9.)

While little is wrong with enjoying some morning brew (especially if you use milk instead of cream or creamer), a lot is wrong if you rely on caffeine instead of food for energy. Be sure to enjoy at least a bagel or granola bar along with the coffee. Also, make the effort to get adequate sleep, so you have less need for a morning caffeine wake-up. The same holds true of tea (which at least contains anti-oxidants, but no energy-providing calories). For a more nourishing hot beverage, enjoy some hot chocolate made with milk or soy milk. And ask for fewer syrup pumps in flavored drinks.

Many young players have developed a "Starbuck's habit." They enjoy the mixed drinks in particular, and often do not associate them as being sources of caffeine. But those drinks do contain caffeine, in addition to potentially enough calories from fat and sugar to equal a small to medium meal (and unhealthful one at that). Understand what you are ordering, and make it a good choice, such as a decaf skim milk latte, or skim milk hot chocolate.

Summary
What you eat in the morning provides fuel for a high-energy day and better soccer playing. Breakfast helps novice and experienced players alike to make their way to the winners' circle. Even dieting soccer players should enjoy breakfast without the fear of "getting fat"—that is, breakfast helps curb evening appetite so that dieters can eat lighter at night.

If you generally skip breakfast, or have only a cup of coffee, tea or juice, at least give breakfast a try for two weeks. You'll soon learn why breakfast is the meal of champions!

Chapter 3
Lunch, Snacks, and Dinner

Whereas breakfast is *the* most important meal of your training diet, lunch is the *second* most important. In fact, Nancy encourages soccer athletes to eat TWO lunches! One lunch at about 11:00 A.M. (or at your break), when you first start to get hungry, then a second lunch at about 3:00 in the afternoon, say, after school, when the munchies strike and there's still time to digest before you start soccer practice at 4:30 or 5:00 P.M. If you train in the morning, these lunches refuel your muscles. If you train in the late afternoon, these lunches prepare you for a strong workout. If you train mid-afternoon, after school, you may want to divide your second lunch into a pre-exercise and a recovery snack. And in all cases, two lunches will curb your appetite so you are not ravenous at the end of the day.

Experiment with this two-lunch concept, especially those many players who seem to go to after-school practices "on empty." If you are like most of Nancy's clients, you'll find yourself looking forward to a second sandwich to boost your energy. Afraid that two lunches will be too much food? Fear not; a second lunch does not mean additional calories. You'll simply be trading your afternoon cookies and evening ice cream for a wholesome afternoon meal. No longer will you crave evening snacks; you will have eaten them earlier (in the form of wholesome foods). And if you want to bulk up, the second lunch offers an opportunity to bolster your calorie intake.

What's for Lunch?

Soccer players commonly have three options for lunch: pack your own, pick up some fast food, or enjoy a hot meal from the deli or cafeteria. You can eat healthfully in each of these scenarios; just remember to enjoy three kinds of wholesome food with each meal (e.g. bread+peanut butter+banana; pizza crust+tomato sauce+cheese; chicken+rice+vegetables) and at least 500 to 600 calories per meal (based on a 2,000 to 2,400 calorie food plan, the amount appropriate for weight-watchers; non-dieters can target about 600 to 800 calories per meal).

Eating a larger hot meal in the middle of the day can make the evening easier if you train in the late afternoon. No longer will you arrive home ravenous, and if you want a smaller dinner, you'll be content to enjoy a simple soup-and-sandwich meal. (For hot lunch suggestions, see the later section on Dinner and Soccer.)

Pack-your-own Lunches

Packing your own lunch is a good way to save money, time, and oftentimes saturated fat and calories *if* you are organized enough to have the right foods on hand. Good nutrition certainly starts in the supermarket. One trick to packing your lunch is to schedule "food shopping." A second trick is to make lunch the night before. Just as we encourage independence among young players (e.g. they should pack and carry their own soccer bag), they should be encouraged to take part in this process. It is one of the many benefits of a great soccer education!

The following suggestions can help you pack a super sports lunch.

- To prevent sandwich bread from getting stale, keep in it the freezer and take out the slices as needed. Bread thaws in minutes at room temperature, or in seconds in the microwave oven.
- Make several sandwiches at one time, and then store them in the freezer. The frozen sandwich will be thawed—and fresh—by lunchtime. Sliced turkey, lean roast beef, peanut butter, and leftover pizza freeze nicely. (Don't freeze eggs, mayonnaise, jelly, lettuce, tomatoes, or raw veggies.)
- Instead of eating a dry sandwich with no mayonnaise, add moistness using lettuce and tomato; low-fat mayonnaise; low-fat bottled salad dressings, such as ranch or creamy Italian; mustard or ketchup.
- Eat peanut butter (or other nut butters); it is a favorite of soccer players, and filled with health-protective fat that reduces your risk of heart disease and diabetes. Enjoy peanut butter (or other nut butters) with sliced banana, raisins, dates, sunflower seeds, apple slices, and/or celery slices.
- Add zip to a cheese sandwich with oregano, Italian seasonings, green peppers, and/or tomatoes.
- Pack leftover soups, chili, and pasta dinners for the next day's lunch. You can either eat the leftovers cold, heat them in a microwave if available, or pack them in thermal containers.

" I enjoy creating my own smoothie for lunch. I whip up some variation of fruit (strawberries, mixed berries, mango, bananas), peanut butter, ice, low-fat and low-sugar vanilla yogurt, and juice or soy milk."

Nicole Barnhart, Goalkeeper, FC Gold Pride
Check out great Smoothies in the Recipe Section!

Going Out for Lunch

Quick-service and family restaurants now offer more low-fat and other healthful foods than ever before. But, you'll still be confronted by the fatty temptations (burgers, fried fish, buttery grilled sandwiches, and French fries) that jump out at you. Before succumbing to grease, remind yourself that you will play better, feel better, and feel *better about yourself* if you eat well.

Here are suggestions for some healthful lunch choices. (Chapter 13 offers additional information.)

Dunkin' Donuts:	Low-fat muffin, bagel, juice, bean or broth-based soups, hot cocoa, bagel and egg-white sandwich
Deli:	Bagel with bean- or broth-based soups; sandwiches or subs with lots of bread and half the roast beef, turkey, ham or cheese. (Or, ask for two extra slices of bread or a second roll to make a sandwich for your second lunch with the excessive meat.) Go light on the mayonnaise, and instead, add moistness with sliced tomatoes, lettuce, mustard or ketchup. Add more carbohydrates with juice, fruit, fig bars, or yogurt for dessert.
McDonald's:	Sandwich with grilled chicken, yogurt parfait, salad with dressing on the side
Wendy's:	Bowl of chili with a plain baked potato
Taco Bell:	Bean burrito
Pizza:	Thick-crust with extra veggies or a side salad rather than extra cheese or pepperoni or other fatty meat
Pasta:	Spaghetti or ziti with tomato sauce and a glass of low-fat milk for protein. Be cautious of lasagna, tortellini, or manicotti that are filled with cheese (i.e., high in saturated fat).
Chinese:	Hot and sour or wonton soup; plain rice with stir-fried entrées such as beef and broccoli or chicken with pea pods. Request the food be cooked with minimal oil. You can also ask for it steamed, which is without any oil. Limit fried appetizers and fried entrées; fill up on steamed rice, instead.
Soups:	Hearty soups (such as split pea, minestrone, lentil, vegetable, or noodle) accompanied by crackers, bread, a plain bagel, or an English muffin provide a satisfying, carbohydrate-rich, low-fat meal.
Beverages:	Both juices and sugar-filled soft drinks are rich in carbohydrates that fuel muscles. Juices, however, are better for your health, providing vitamin C, potassium, and overall nutritional quality.

Salad for Lunch

Salads, whether served as a main dish or an accompaniment, are a simple way to boost your intake of fresh vegetables—that's good! But as a soccer athlete, you need a substantial, carbohydrate-based lunch. Most salads get the bulk of their calories from salad oil—not good. You'll be better able to fuel your muscles if you choose a sandwich with a side salad for lunch, rather then eat just a big salad for the entire meal. However, if a salad is your choice, to make it a meal, make sure to add from the substantial choices below.

Three tricks to making a healthy sports salad are:
1. Choose a variety of colorful vegetables—dark green lettuces, red tomatoes, yellow peppers, orange carrots—for a variety of vitamins and minerals. If the vegetables you buy for salads tend to wilt in your refrigerator, consider frequent trips to the salad bar at the grocery store and deli as an alternative to tossing veggies that spoil before you find the chance to eat them. And here's a tip: dig from the bottom, to make sure to get the coldest (and therefore best preserved) part of the salad bar.

2. Add extra carbohydrates, or protein:
   • dense vegetables, such as corn, peas, beets, carrots
   • beans and legumes, such as chickpeas, kidney beans, and three-bean salad
   • cooked rice or pasta
   • oranges, apples, raisins, grapes, craisins
   • toasted croutons
   • whole-grain bread or roll on the side
   • hardboiled eggs, cheese (moderate amounts), chicken, flaked tuna or imitation seafood, preferably without mayonnaise. (If it comes with mayo, hold off adding any extra dressing to the salad or add lemon or vinegar.)

3. Monitor the dressing. Some soccer players drown 50 calories of healthful salad ingredients with 400 calories of blue cheese dressing! At a restaurant, always request the dressing be served on the side. Otherwise, you may get 400 calories of unhealthy oil, or mayonnaise—fatty foods that fill your stomach but leave your muscles unfueled.

If you choose to use regular dressings, try to select ones made with olive oil for both a nice flavor and health-protective monounsaturated fats. If you want to reduce your fat intake, simply dilute regular dressings with water, more vinegar, lemon, or even milk (in ranch and other mayonnaise-based dressings). Or, choose from the plethora of low- or non-fat salad dressings. These dressings are good not only for salads, but also sandwiches, baked potatoes, and dips.

Salads

Here are how some popular salad ingredients compare. Note that the ones with the most color generally have the most nutritional value. Remember some other nutritional powerhouse additions that are usually part of the salad bar: beans (garbanzo, kidney), beets, carrots, cauliflower, imitation seafood, chicken or tuna (all preferably without mayo or other dressing: add your own).

Salad Ingredient	Daily Value	Vitamin C (mg) 60 mg	Vitamin A (IU) 5,000 IU	Magnesium (mg) 400 mg
Broccoli, 5" stalk	(180 g)	110	2,500	24
Green pepper, $1/2$	(70 g)	65	210	20
Spinach, 2 cups raw	(110 g)	50	8,100	90
Tomato, medium	(12 g)	25	760	15
Romaine, 2 cups	(110 g)	30	3,000	10
Iceberg, 2 cups	(110 g)	5	360	5
Cucumber, $1/2$ medium	(150 g)	10	325	15
Celery, 1 stalk	(40 g)	5	55	4

Solving the Four O'clock Munchies

Many athletes believe eating in the afternoon is sinful. They self-inflict "Thou shalt not snack" as an Eleventh Commandment. Then, if they succumb, they feel guilty. Or more likely, younger players do not plan for after-school eating, and then train on empty. Hunger is neither bad nor wrong. It is a normal physiological function. You can expect to get hungry every four hours. If you have lunch at 11:00 or 12:00 P.M., your body needs fuel by 3:00 or 4:00 P.M.

If you think of your afternoon fuel as a "second lunch," you'll end up with wholesome food—a second sandwich, a mug of soup, or peanut butter on crackers and a (decaf) latte. In comparison, "afternoon snack" suggests candy, cookies and sweets—the goodies craved by soccer players who eat too little at breakfast and first lunch. The preferred solution to sweet cravings is to prevent the cravings by eating more food earlier in the day, and having a second lunch later in the afternoon. The second lunch maintains afternoon energy and helps prevent evening over-eating.

"When I was on the Boston Breakers, Nancy taught us to eat two lunches. It's good to eat the same amount of food four times a day instead of a little bit in the morning and then a lot towards the end of the day."

Amy Rodriguez, Forward, Philadelphia Independence

Second Lunch Suggestions

Some players enjoy a second sandwich for their second lunch. But others like to graze on two or three wholesome snacks from this list. If you carry snacks with you, or keep a supply of "emergency food" in your soccer bag or your parents' car that's ready and waiting for the afternoon (or anytime) munchies, you can avoid the temptations that lurk in every convenience store, vending machine, or bakery. Try to pick items from two or three different food groups, such as carrots + cottage cheese + crackers; or graham crackers + peanut butter + apple. This ensures you've created a balanced snack to last you for the "long run."

Perishable snacks to carry with you or buy fresh:	Nonperishable snacks to keep stocked in your locker or soccer bag:
• whole wheat bagel	• cold cereal (by the handful or bowlful with milk)
• low-fat bran muffin	• hot cereal (packets of instant oatmeal)
• microwaved potato or sweet potato/yam	• reduced-fat microwave popcorn
• yogurt, low-fat	• canned soup
• cottage cheese, low-fat	• canned tuna
• cheese sticks, low-fat	• low-fat crackers (Ak-Mak, Wasa, Melba Toast)
• thick-crust pizza	• graham crackers
• fresh fruit	• low-fat granola bars
• baby carrots	• energy bars
• leftover pasta	• juice boxes or bottles
• frozen meal	• dried fruit
• peanut butter sandwich	• peanut butter
• hard boiled egg	• nuts, trail mix

Snack Attack

Here are some fun soccer snack ideas:

Avocado chip mini sandwiches. Chips are salty and spicy enough on their own to accommodate plain avocado (as opposed to guacamole or other dip), and this is easy. Put avocado pieces between large chips, and serve as appetizers.

A Healthier S'more: Yael Averbuch of Sky Blue FC loves dark chocolate. She invented spreading squares of dark chocolate with peanut butter; try a little cinnamon on it too. It's great on its own, but you can also try it between graham crackers.

Frozen Fruit. Blueberries, strawberries, grapes, oranges—all make fun and flavorful snacks when eaten right from the freezer.

Frozen yogurt cups. Buy blended flavors, put containers in freezer. A healthier alternative to an ice cream treat, it defrosts on the road and can be eaten thawed.

Vending machine or tournament snacks: Vending-machine cuisine, which resembles choices at tournaments, offers tough choices. But tucked among the lackluster choices, you may be able to find pretzels, peanuts, juice, yogurt, or even an apple. The good part about vending-machine snacks is that they are limited in size (e.g., only three cookies instead of the whole bag) and generally provide only 200 to 400 calories, not 2,000.

If you're trying to decide between fatty or sugary choices (i.e., chips vs. jelly beans), remember that the sugar in jelly beans will appropriately fuel your muscles, whereas the fat in the chips will clog the arteries. (After eating a sugary snack, be sure to brush or rinse your teeth.) Tournaments often sell candy bars and M & M's. Try to be equipped with better options so these don't become your only choice.

Sweet treats: If it's cookies, brownies, an ice cream sundae, or any other such treat that you crave once a week or so, Nancy recommends you satisfy your hankering by enjoying the treat. You won't destroy your health with an occasional treat, as long as your overall diet tends to be wholesome, and as long as you eat it at a time that will not hurt your performance. You can still maintain a diet that averages 90% quality foods, 10% treats.

Sweets, treats, and fast foods are best saved for after the games. This was a vow Gloria's teams young players made among themselves. Remember, you eat for yourself to enhance performance, and you do it for your team as well.

Healthful snacks and munchies: To reduce the temptation of the vending machine or tournament choices, keep handy in your soccer bag, locker or car a supply of wholesome options: whole-grain bagels, crackers, pretzels, fig bars, energy bars, granola bars, oatmeal-raisin cookies, graham crackers, raisins and other dried fruit, trail mix, V-8 juice, and juice boxes.

Dinner and Soccer

Dinnertime generally marks the end of the school or work day, a time to relax and enjoy a pleasant meal, that is, if you (or your parents) have the energy to prepare it—and if your soccer practice or game is not in the middle of the family dinner hour. (Many families rearrange their meal times to accommodate hungry soccer players.) The trick to dining on a balanced dinner—the protein-starch-vegetable kind of meal with at least three kinds of foods—is to arrive home with enough *energy* to prepare it. This means fueling your body and brain with adequate calories prior to dinnertime—with a second lunch, or a post-soccer snack on the way home. It also means having easy-to-heat food ready and waiting. A cook-a-thon on a weekend can simplify weekday dinners.

If you are far from being a master chef, you might want to take a cooking class at your local center for adult education. It might be a fun activity for soccer parents and/or their players. But even if you're not a good cook, being organized can still produce a great sports diet.

Quick Fixes: Dinner Tips for Hungry Soccer Players

Because good nutrition starts in the supermarket, you have a far better chance of achieving a super sports diet when your kitchen is well stocked with appropriate foods. You (or your parents) might want to muster up enough energy to marathon shop at the discount or warehouse food store once every two or three weeks and *really shop*, so that you have enough food to last for a while. To help accomplish this goal, post a copy of the *Soccer Player's Basic Shopping List* (see following sidebar) on your refrigerator and check off the foods you need.

Soccer Player's Basic Shopping List

Keep this on your refrigerator and be sure to notice when an item gets low and needs to be replaced.

Cupboard: cereal, spaghetti, spaghetti sauce, brown rice, whole grain crackers, baked corn chips, kidney beans, baked beans, refried beans, tuna (canned or in a foil pouch), salmon (canned or in a foil pouch), peanut butter, soups (such as mushroom for making casseroles; lentil, minestrone, hearty bean), baking potatoes, V-8 or other vegetable juices

Refrigerator: low-fat cheddar, mozzarella and cottage cheese, low-fat milk and (Greek) yogurt, Parmesan cheese, eggs, tofu, tortillas, carrots, lettuce, tomatoes, oranges, bananas (When refrigerated, the banana peel turns black but the fruit itself is fine and lasts longer.)

Freezer: whole-grain bagels, whole-wheat pita, English muffins, multigrain bread, orange juice concentrate, broccoli, spinach, winter squash, ground turkey, extra-lean hamburger, chicken (pieces frozen individually in baggies)

By keeping your kitchen well stocked with basic foods, you will have the makings for simple meals such as:

- Spaghetti with tomato sauce plus hamburger, ground turkey, tofu, beans, cheese cottage, grated cheese, and/or vegetables
- English muffin or pita pizzas
- Tuna noodle casserole
- Soup and sandwiches (e.g. tuna, toasted cheese, peanut butter with banana)
- Microwaved potato topped with cottage or ricotta cheese, baked beans, or yogurt
- Peanut butter crackers and V-8 juice
- Bean burritos (frozen, or made with canned refried beans+salsa+tortilla)

Some soccer players use their morning shower time to cook $1^1/_2$ cups of raw (brown) rice while getting ready for work. Come dinnertime, they simply brown one pound of lean hamburger or ground turkey in a large skillet, dump in the cooked rice, and then add whatever vegetable is handy. Cooking $1^1/_2$ cups of raw rice for each pound of raw lean meat generates two generous sports meals with 60% of the calories from carbohydrates. Perfect!

Some popular creations with rice and ground meat include:

- Mexican—canned beans + chili powder + grated low-fat Cheddar cheese + diced tomatoes
- Chinese—broccoli zapped in the microwave oven while the meat cooks + soy sauce
- Italian—green beans + Italian seasonings such as basil, oregano, and garlic powder
- American—grated low-fat Cheddar cheese + onion browned with the meat + diced tomatoes

Quick and Easy Meal Ideas

Here are some ideas for quick-and-easy meals:
- pasta with clam sauce, tomato sauce, and/or frozen vegetables, and/or lowfat cheese
- canned beans, rinsed and then spooned over rice, pasta, or salads
- frozen dinners, supplemented with whole-grain bread and fresh fruit
- Pierogies, tortellini, and burritos from the frozen food section
- baked potato topped with cottage cheese or ricotta
- whole-grain cereal (hot or cold) with fruit and low-fat milk
- quick-cooking brown rice — made double for the next day's rice and bean salad
- stir-fry, using precut vegetables from the market, salad bar, or freezer. Purchase garlic sauce at any take-out Chinese restaurant (and rice too if you need it) and add to your own cooked vegetables, rice, leftrover meats.
- Scrambled eggs (Combine beaten eggs and seasonings with grated raw zucchini, cheese, tomato slices, or leftover coked vegetables.)
- thick-crust pizza, fresh or frozen, then reheated in the toaster oven
- homemade pizza (pizza dough from the supermarket with jarred spaghetti sauce, steamed vegetables, and grated cheese)
- bean soups, homemade, canned, or from the deli
- souped-up soup (canned soup with added steamed vegetables, leftover meat, fish or grated cheese)

Pasta and Soccer

Every soccer player regardless of language understands the word *pasta*. Pasta is popular not only before a game, but also as a standard part of the training diet. Even soccer players who claim they can't cook can manage to boil pasta. Some choose to eat pasta at least five nights of the week thinking it is a kind of superfood. Wrong.

Granted, pasta is carbohydrate-rich, quick and easy to cook, heart-healthy, economical, fun to eat, and enjoyed by just about every member of the family. But in terms of vitamins, minerals, and protein, plain pasta is a lackluster food. Here's some information to help you to place pasta in perspective.

Nutritional value: Pasta is an excellent source of carbohydrates for muscle fuel, and is the equivalent of "gas" for your engine. But plain pasta is a marginal source of vitamins and minerals, the "spark plugs" you need for good health. Pasta is simply made from refined white flour—the same stuff you get in "wonder breads"—with a few vitamins added to replace those lost during processing. Even whole-wheat pastas—although better than white for their fiber content—offer little nutritional superiority, because wheat (and other grains in general) is better respected for its carbohydrate-value than its vitamins and minerals. Spinach and tomato pastas also get overrated since they contain relatively little spinach or tomato in comparison to having a serving of that vegetable along with the meal.

Pasta's nutritional value comes primarily from the sauces:
- tomato and pesto-type sauces rich in vitamins A and C and potassium
- clam sauce rich in protein, zinc, and iron

Be cautious with pasta smothered with butter, cream, or greasy meat sauces. Creamy, cheesy pastas are artery-clogging nutritional nightmares.

Pasta and protein: Pasta is popular not only for carbohydrates but also for being a vegetarian alternative to meat-based meals. However, many soccer players—often non-meat eaters—live on *too much* pasta and neglect their protein needs. To boost the protein-content of tomato sauce, add:
- 2-3 ounces of extra-lean ground beef or turkey
- $1/4$ cup of grated low-fat mozzarella cheese

- $^1/_2$ cake tofu
- $^1/_2$ cup canned, drained kidney, black or garbanzo beans
- 3 ounces tuna (one-half of a 6-ounce can)
- $^1/_2$ cup of canned minced clams, shrimp or other fish
- 1 cup of low-fat cottage or ricotta cheese
- Nuts (walnuts, almonds, cashews, peanuts)
- Sauces made with protein sources, such as peanut, tahini (sesame paste), yogurt

Or, instead of adding protein to the sauce, drink two glasses of low-fat milk with the meal.

To boost the nutritional content even further, make a Vegetable Pesto Sauce: Puree cooked broccoli, carrots or other cooked vegetables in a food processor or blender. Use a bit of chicken or vegetable stock for the desired consistency. Season to taste. You can make this in batches, freeze it in ice cube trays, and store the cubes in freezer bags for convenient use.

Summary

If you are like many soccer players who struggle with eating well on a daily basis, remember the following keys to a successful sports diet:

1. Eat appropriately sized meals on a regular schedule so that you won't get too hungry. Notice how your lunches and dinner deteriorate when you eat too little breakfast and get too hungry.

2. Spend your calories on a *variety* of wholesome foods at each meal; target at least three kinds of food per meal.

3. Pay attention to how much better you feel, perform, and feel about yourself when you eat a well-balanced sports diet.

Nancy believes that *getting too hungry* is the biggest mistake with most soccer players' diets, especially if you have not planned ahead and get stuck with few or no good food choices. A hearty breakfast sets the stage for a top-notch sports diet, and a second lunch that prevents the hungry horrors paves the way to a healthful dinner.

Chapter 4
Vitamins and Supplements for Soccer Players

Vitamins are essential food components that your body can't make. They perform important jobs, including helping to convert food into energy. (Vitamins do not provide energy, however.) As a hungry athlete who requires more food than the average person, you can easily consume large doses of vitamins in, for example, a taller glass of orange juice or bigger plate of steamed broccoli. (Chapter 1 has information about some of the best food sources of vitamins.)

Because food consumption surveys suggest that many people fail to eat a well-balanced variety of wholesome foods, some soccer players may indeed suffer from marginal nutritional deficiencies, particularly those who restrict calories or skimp on fruits, vegetables, and dairy foods. Yet despite the rising popularity of supplements, most health organizations, including the American Heart Association and the National Institutes of Health, recommend food, not pills, for optimal nutrition. That's because whole food is comprised of far more than just vitamins. It contains carbohydrates, protein, phytochemicals, fiber, and other health-protective substances that are not in pills, and interact in ways that cannot necessarily be duplicated by pills. Hence, the key to good health is to learn how to eat well, regardless of your busy lifestyle, and to teach young athletes not to focus on getting everything in pills.

Get nutrition from food first, but by all means get it!
Getting nutrients from food is first choice. If you fail to do that, supplements are an option, but it's naïve to think that a pill can replace food. For example, many soccer players fail to consume a calcium-rich food at each meal, so they come up short on the recommended calcium intake. They drink plenty of water and sports drinks, but we rarely, if ever, see athletes drinking milk other than on just breakfast cereal.

Even young children are falling short. According to the USDA, nearly a third of children under age five don't receive adequate calcium. By adolescence, the figure is stunning: 88% of girls ages 12 to 19 and 68% of boys the same age fail to get enough. And don't forget the importance of milk fortified with Vitamin D. FC Gold Pride defender Rachel Buehler, a standout Stanford graduate and pre-med candidate, points out, "Studies have linked vitamin D to proper immune system function, cancer prevention and cardiovascular disease prevention to name a few. It is also crucial for calcium absorption, which is necessary for strong bones. Although it was once believed that most people synthesize enough vitamin D as a result of sun exposure, recent research shows that that is not actually the case, and many people do not get enough."

The bottom line: be responsible and enjoy 100 to 150 calories of a calcium-rich food at each meal (for example, milk on cereal, yogurt with lunch, chocolate milk for a recovery snack, and milk with dinner). If for whatever reason you are unable to do that, a calcium+Vitamin D supplement is a second-best option that offers calcium and D, despite the fact it offers none of the other life-sustaining nutrients found in a whole food.

Soccer players who eat vitamin-enriched foods such as energy bars and breakfast cereals commonly consume far more vitamins than they realize. But take note: soccer players who eat primarily "all natural foods" from the whole food stores miss out on the benefit of enriched foods—added vitamins or minerals, such as B-vitamins and iron. That's one reason why the government food guidelines acknowledge that some of our grains can appropriately come from enriched foods.

> *"I start off every day with a bowl of Total Cereal, because I know it's fortified with iron and is a very easy way for me to boost my iron intake."*

Amy Rodriguez, Forward, Philadelphia Independence

To date, no studies have documented a physiological need for mega-doses of vitamins for soccer players or other athletes who train hard. Yet, supplements are indeed appropriate for certain populations, including:

- folic acid for pregnant women and women who *might* become pregnant (expectedly or unexpectedly), to prevent certain birth defects.
- iron for vegetarians and females with heavy menstrual periods.
- vitamin D for people who get very little sunlight (gymnasts, ice hockey players, those in less sunny climates).

If you choose to take a supplement for "health insurance" and for any potential health-protective effects, be sure to do so *in addition to eating well*. Researchers have yet to unravel the entire vitamin/health mystery, so stay tuned and be sure to take care of your whole health with the vitamins, phytochemicals, omega-3 fats, and other unknown, but important, substances found in whole foods.

Vitamins for Fatigue?

Some soccer players complain of chronic fatigue. They feel run down, dragged out, and overwhelmingly exhausted. They come to Nancy wondering if something is wrong with their diet—and if taking vitamins would solve the problem. Here are some questions she asks to help decipher the source of their energy problems.

- *Are you tired due to low blood sugar?* If you skimp on breakfast, miss lunch because you "don't have time" and then doze off in the afternoon because you have low blood sugar, no amount of vitamins will solve that energy problem! You need to *choose* to make time to eat lunch, and *choose* to stock wholesome snacks (nuts, dried fruit) at school or work.

- *Is your diet too low in carbohydrates?* If you eat too many fast-but-fatty food choices, or you think just salad with chicken is a healthy choice, you will fill your stomach but leave your muscles poorly fueled with inadequate glycogen to support your training program. You'll end up playing with "dead legs."

- *Are you eating enough?* Some female soccer players simply don't eat enough, and/or enough of the right foods. They erroneously buy into the diets of sedentary peers, or they are too distracted or busy to consider fueling to be equally important as training.

"If I don't eat enough, then obviously I feel a tired and sluggish. I've learned to always make sure I get enough fuel into my system."

Kelly Smith, Forward, Boston Breakers

- *Are you iron-deficient and anemic?* If you eat little red meat and consequently consume little iron, you might be low in this important mineral in red blood cells that helps carry oxygen to exercising muscles. Iron-deficiency anemia can result in needless fatigue during exercise. (To boost your dietary iron intake, with or without meat, see Chapter 7.) You might also want to talk with your doctor about getting your blood tested (hemoglobin, hematocrit, ferritin, serum iron, and total iron-binding capacity) to rule out the possibility of anemia.

FEMALE PLAYERS AND IRON

There are cases in which female soccer players, even as an entire team, undergo simple blood tests to determine iron levels. And when and if there is a shortage, iron supplements may be prescribed. This is the case for Sonia Bompastor, a 2009 leaguewide Player of the Month from the Washington Freedom, who relates,

"I take iron because I'm anemic and I need that iron to perform on the field. If I don't take the pills my body is tired and I always want to sleep. A lot of soccer players need to take iron."

- *Are you getting enough sleep?* Perhaps you are simply burning the candle at both ends and are rightfully tired. While advice to "get more sleep" is easier said than done, you can strive to make sleep more of a priority on your "to do" list.

THE NEED FOR SLEEP

In addition to fatigue, lack of sleep directly affects athletic performance. According to research by Peter Walters, Assistant Professor of Kinesiology at Wheaton College in Illinois, cumulative sleep deprivation has been shown to reduce cardiovascular performance by 11%. It also affects other measures of performances, such as focus, perceived exertion, and alters the supply of energy to the muscles.

- *Are you overtraining?* Some soccer players think they will improve faster if they train as hard as possible every day. Wrong! One or two rest days or easy days per week are an essential part of a training program; rest days provide the time the body needs to replenish depleted muscle glycogen. This can be difficult with mostly organized play and overcrowded scheduling. Look for a coach/team with a sensible program; talk to your current coach, and don't double card (play for two teams) or guest play if you suspect overtraining, or don't want to risk it.

- *Are you stressed or depressed?* When life is feeling out of control, stresses can certainly drain your mental energy, create sleep problems, and leave you feeling exhausted. Choosing to eat healthful meals on a regular schedule can help you feel better both physically and mentally. That is energizing in itself. Food increases the level of serotonin, the "feel good" hormone.

For most soccer players, resolving fatigue with better eating, sleeping, and training habits is more effective than taking vitamin pills. By implementing the simple food suggestions in this book, you can transform low-energy eating patterns into a fueling plan for success.

Summary

Your best bet for fighting fatigue is to be responsible with your choices and nourish your body with the right balance of wholesome foods. Make the effort to eat a variety of foods and fluids from the different food groups every day to consume not only the amount of the vitamins and minerals you need, but also the *calories* your body needs to prevent fatigue.

If you are tempted to take supplements for health insurance, do so only if you simultaneously choose to eat responsibly. Remember, no amount of supplements will compensate for an inadequate diet—but you will *always* win with good nutrition. Eat wisely, eat well!

For more Information

Confusion abounds regarding dietary supplements, their safety, and their potential health benefits. Here are some websites that offer abundant information about vitamins and health. (You might need to do a search on "vitamins" or "fish oil" to find your topic of interest).

The American Heart Association:
www.americanheart.org

FDA's Center for Food Safety and Applied Nutrition:
www.cfsan.fda.gov

National Library of Medicine:
www.nlm.nih.gov/medlineplus

The World's Healthiest Foods:
www.whfoods.org

SECTION II

CARBS, PROTEIN, FATS AND FLUIDS—THE RIGHT BALANCE

Chapter 5
Carbohydrates: The Fundamental Fuel

As a soccer athlete, you need carbohydrates to fuel your muscles (to delay fatigue) and feed your brain (to help you concentrate). You can consume carbs by eating fruits, vegetables, grains, and any form of starch or sugar, be it bananas, (brown) rice, pasta, potatoes, honey, sports drinks, hard candy, even marshmallows. Obviously, you'll enhance your health if you choose carbs primarily from fruits, vegetables, and whole grains. But the sugary foods do offer the "gas" that instantly fuels your muscles. The sugars just fail to offer any health protective vitamins or minerals.

Questions abound about the role of carbohydrates in the sports diet. The purpose of this chapter is to address carbohydrate confusion and provide some clarity for soccer players who want to eat wisely for good health, high energy, weight control and top performance.

Q. How much carbohydrate should I eat?
A. Research with soccer players suggests:
- The average soccer player with moderate calorie needs should target about 2 to 3 grams of carb per pound body weight (5 to 7 g carb/kg). This means:

If you weigh:	Total #g carb/day	Target #g carbs per meal: (Breakfast, Lunch, Lunch #2, Dinner)
100 lbs (45 kg)	200 to 300 g	50 to 75 g
125 lbs (57 kg)	250 to 375 g	60 to 95 g
150 lbs (68 kg)	300 to 450 g	80 to 110 g
175 lbs (80 kg)	350 to 525 g	90 to 130 g

Sample 50 gram carbohydrate choices

Here are some examples of what 50 grams (200 calories) of carbohydrate "looks like." Be sure to consume enough carbs, making them the foundation of each meal and snack.

Wheaties, 2 cups • Nature Valley Granola Bar, 1.5 packets (3 bars) • Thomas' Bagel, 1 (3.5 oz) • Banana, 2 medium • Orange juice, 16 ounces • Apple, 2 medium • Raisins, 1/2 cup • Pepperidge Farm multi-grain bread, 2.5 slices • Baked potato, 1 large (6.5 ounces) • Pasta, 1 cup cooked • Rice, 1 cup cooked • Fig Newtons, 5 • Flavored Yogurt + 3 graham cracker squares

- The serious soccer player with high calorie needs due to numerous workouts and intense practices and games should target about 4 to 5 grams of carb per pound body weight (8 to 10 g carb/kg). This means, if you weigh 120 pounds (55 kg), you should target about 500 to 600 g carb (about 2,000 to 2,400 calories of carb) per day. That's a lot of pasta and juice!

To consume that much carbohydrate, you really need to eat carbs as the foundation of every meal and snack: cereal for breakfast; sandwiches made with hearty breads for lunch; bananas and bagels for snacks; and pasta for dinner. The benefit will be better-fueled muscles that enable you to:

- perform with greater intensity. Elite players may have 150 to 250 brief bursts of intense action during a game. (Bangsbo). Players with low glycogen tend to walk more and sprint less—about 33% less. (Balsom)
- cover more distance at the end of the game. Studies of soccer players with low glycogen suggest they covered 25% less distance in the second half of the game. (Ekblom)
- delay fatigue. When your glygocen stores are low, you'll experience extreme fatigue. (Bangsbo)

Q. Aren't carbs fattening? Shouldn't I eat less of them so I can be a lean soccer player?

A. No! Carbohydrates are not inherently fattening. Excess *calories* are fattening. Excess calories of carbohydrates (bread, bagels, pasta) are actually less fattening than are excess calories of fat (butter, mayonnaise, frying oils) because the body has to spend calories to convert excess carbohydrates into body fat. In comparison, the body easily converts excess dietary fat into body fat. This means if you are destined to be gluttonous but want to suffer the least weight gain, you might want to indulge in (high carb) frozen yogurt instead of (high fat) gourmet ice cream.

Q. If carbs aren't fattening, why do high protein diets "work"?

A. High protein diets seemingly "work" because—

1. The dieter loses water weight. Carbs hold water in the muscles. For each ounce of carbohydrate you store as glycogen, your body simultaneously stores about three ounces of water. When you exercise, your body releases the water.
2. People eliminate calories when they stop eating carbohydrates. For example, you might eliminate not only the baked potato (200 calories) but also two pats of butter (100 calories) on top of the potato—and this creates a calorie deficit.
3. Protein tends to be more satiating than is carbohydrate. That is, protein (and fat) lingers longer in the stomach than does carbohydrate. Hence, having 200 calories from three protein-rich eggs for breakfast will satiate you longer than 200 calories from two slices of high carb toast with jam. By curbing hunger, you have fewer urges to eat and can more easily restrict calories—that is, until you start to crave carbs and over-eat them. (You know the scene: "Last chance

to eat bread before I go back on my diet, so I'd better eat the whole loaf now...")

The overwhelming reason why high protein diets do NOT work is people fail to stay on them forever. Remember: You should never start a food program you do not want to maintain for the rest of your life. Do you really want never to eat breads, potato or crackers ever again? Your better option is to learn how to manage carbs, not avoid them. Also, these types of diets are not good for young athletes, for performance reasons, lack of balanced eating and for the message they communicate that normal eating is "not okay."

Q. Is there a difference between the carbs in starchy foods (like breads) vs. the carbs in fruits and vegetables or in candy?

A. As far as your muscles are concerned, there is no difference. You can carbo-load on gummy bears, bananas or brown rice; they are biochemically similar. Sugars and starches both offer the same amount of energy (4 calories per gram, or 16 calories per teaspoon) and both can get stored as glycogen in muscles or used for fuel by the brain (via the blood sugar).

The sugar in jelly beans is a simple compound, one or two molecules linked together. The starch in (brown) rice is a complex compound with hundreds to thousands of sugar molecules linked together. Sugars can convert into starches and starches can convert into sugars. For example, a green (not ripe) banana is starchy. A ripe banana becomes sweeter; in fruits, the starch converts into sugar. Peas are sweet when they are young. As they get older, they get starchier; in vegetables, the sugar converts into starch.

Grain foods (wheat, rice, corn, oats) also store their energy as complex strands of sugar molecules, a starch. The starch breaks down into individual sugar molecules (glucose) during digestion. Hence, your muscles don't care if you eat sugars or starches for fuel because they both digest into the same simple sugar: glucose.

The difference between sugars and starches comes in their nutritional value and impact on your health. Some sugars and starches are healthier than others. For example, the sugar in orange juice is accompanied by vitamin C, folate and potassium. The sugar in orange soda pop is void of vitamins and minerals; that's why it's described as "empty calories." The starch in whole wheat bread is accompanied by fiber and phytochemicals. The starch in white breads has lost many health protective nutrients during the refining process.

Q. Is white bread "poison"?

A. White bread offers lackluster nutrition, but it is not "poison" nor a "bad" food. White bread can be balanced into an overall wholesome diet (as can pasta and other foods made from refined while flour). That is, if you have whole grain cereal for breakfast and brown rice for dinner, your diet can healthfully accommodate a sandwich made on white bread for lunch. White breads and food made from refined flour tend to be enriched with B-vitamins, iron and folate—all important nutrients for soccer players. According to the U.S. Dietary Guidelines, about half of your grain choices can appropriately be refined, enriched grains.

Q. Is sugar "evil"?

A. Sugar is fuel, not evil. While the sugar in oranges and other fruits is accompanied by important vitamins and minerals, the sugar in, for example, candy or soda is void of nutritional value. In general, Nancy suggests athletes limit their refined sugar intake to about 10% of total calories. That's about 200 to 300 calories of sugar per day; 200 calories equates to either a quart of Gatorade, two sports gels, 16 ounces of soda pop, or 10 jelly beans.

Most athletes can handle sugar just fine. But for a few, sugar seems "evil" because it contributes to swings in blood sugar levels that can result in feeling lightheaded and shaky. If you are "sugar sensitive" and notice that sugar makes you feel bad, if you eat sugar, have it along with protein, such as jelly with peanut butter, or fruit flavored yogurt with almonds.

Q. Should I avoid sugar pre-exercise?

A. The best advice regarding pre-exercise sugar is for you to *avoid the desire for sugar* by having eaten appropriately prior to exercise. For example, if you crave sugar before an afternoon soccer practice, you could have prevented the desire for sugary, quick-energy foods by having eaten a bigger breakfast and lunch. Sugar cravings can be a sign you have gotten too hungry.

Note that sugar taken *during* exercise is unlikely to contribute to a hypoglycemic reaction because muscles quickly use the sugar without the need for extra insulin. This includes sports drinks, gels, sports beans, gummy candies and other popular sugary choices. (See Chapter 10 for more advice about pre-exercise fueling.)

Q. *Should I choose foods based on their glycemic effect/glycemic index (that is, the rate at which they cause blood sugar to increase)?*
A. Not necessarily. The glycemic response to a food varies from person to person, as well as from meal to meal (depending on the combinations of foods you eat). You'll be better off experimenting with a variety of grains, fruits, and vegetables to learn what food combinations settle well, satisfy your appetite and offer lasting energy. Some choices, however, are obvious. Players have been known to "crash" midgame on a breakfast of a can of soda versus one of oatmeal.

Wholesome, fiber-rich fruits, vegetables, beans and whole grains are wise food choices because they tend to have a low glycemic effect (that is, cause a slow rise in blood sugar) and they are nutrient-dense, can curb your appetite and may even help with weight management.

What are Some Examples of Carb-based Meals?

While you can get some carbs from fruits and vegetables, most soccer players do not get enough carbs from these foods alone. Here are a few suggestions for carb-based meals:

Breakfast: raisin bran, Grape-Nuts, granola and other cold cereals, oatmeal, bagels, muffins, pancakes, waffles, English muffins, toast, French toast

Lunch: sandwiches made on hearty wholesome breads; hearty soups with beans, lentils, pasta; vegetable pizza with thick crust

Dinner: meals with pasta, potato, rice, noodles, or other grains covering most of the plate; extra vegetables; rolls or bread

Snacks and accompaniments to the meals: fruit juice, bananas, fruit smoothies, dried fruit, pretzels, baked chips, fig cookies, flavored yogurt, frozen yogurt, hot cocoa/chocolate milk

Be sure also to include some protein as an accompaniment to the carbs. While carbs fuel the muscles, protein builds and repairs muscles. The next chapter offers more details about the right balance of carbs and protein. Keep reading!

GO WITH GRAINS

In addition to rice (brown is preferable, since it has more fiber and nutritional value than white rice), try other grain varieties, such as quinoa (KEEN-wah, tastes like a grain, but it is technically a protein), barley, millet, couscous, buckwheat etc. Cook a large amount to have leftovers. Here are some ways to Go with Grains.

Sweet grains: cook with, or toss in cranberries or raisins when grains are done but still steaming, to plump them up. Add nuts or seeds.

Make a grain loaf or burgers: cooked grains combined with eggs, cheese, ground nuts and seeds then baked or sautéed.

Make a grain based salad, by mixing in any and all vegetables.
Toss in salty feta cheese (good for hot weather and sodium needs) or other cheese.

Use leftover cooked grains to make a breakfast porridge. Add milk and cook until soft.
Sweeten with fruit, raisins and/or honey or brown sugar.

See the Recipe Section for additional grain ideas.

Summary

Carbohydrates should not be a source of confusion. To the contrary: wholesome carbs—fruits, vegetables, and grains—clearly should be the foundation of your sports diet. You need them to fuel your muscles so you can be strong all the way to the end of the game.

As a soccer player, you may be unable to get adequate carbs from fruits and vegetables to fuel your muscles, so be sure to include pasta, potato, rice or other starch in your meal menu. Limit your intake of refined carbs—soda pop, sugar, and sports drinks—because they lack health-promoting nutrients. By "carbo-loading" every day, your muscles will have the fuel they need to train at their best. This will help you recover quickly, feel good, and enjoy your practices and games.

Chapter 6
Protein for Muscles

Between ads for protein supplements and the false rumors about carbs being fattening, many soccer players and their parents wrongly believe protein should be the foundation of their sports diets. While you do need adequate protein, it should be an accompaniment to the carb-based meals that fuel your muscles. Smaller amounts of protein—about 10% to 15% of your calories—can adequately build and repair muscles, make red blood cells, enzymes and hormones, and allow hair and fingernails to grow. This translates into a small-to-medium portion of protein at each meal.

How Much Protein is Enough?

For a serious soccer player, an adequate and safe protein intake is about 0.5 to 0.8 grams per pound of body weight (1.2 to 1.7 g/kg). This means:
- A 120-pound (55 kg) female soccer player needs approximately 60 to 95 grams of protein per day.
- A 160-pound (73 kg) male player needs about 80 to 130 grams of protein. The sidebar below "How to Balance Your Protein Intake" can help you calculate your protein needs and compare your needs to what you actually consume. This protein recommendation is based on the assumptions:
- You are eating plenty of calories. (Your protein needs increase if you are dieting. That's because some protein gets burned for fuel rather than gets used to build or protect muscles.)
- Your muscles are well fueled with carbohydrates. (You'll burn more protein for fuel if your muscles become glycogen depleted.)

Although avid soccer players need more protein than do sedentary people, this higher requirement generally does not translate into larger portions. Most people (including soccer players) typically consume more than the recommended protein intake. (Burke)

How to Balance Your Protein Intake

If you wonder if you are eating too little (or too much) protein, you can estimate your daily protein needs by multiplying your weight (or a good weight for your body) by 0.5 to 0.8 grams of protein per pound (1.2 to 1.7 g pro/kg).

Weight in lbs (kg)	Protein (grams/day)
100 (45)	50-80
120 (55)	60-90
150 (68)	75-100
170 (77)	85-115

Use food labels and the chart on the next page to calculate your protein intake. Pay close attention to portion sizes!

Approximate Protein Content of Some Commonly Eaten Foods

Animal Proteins	Protein (g)
Beef, 4 ounces, (120 g) cooked*	32
Chicken breast, 4 ounces (120 g) cooked	32
Tuna, 1 can (6.5 ounces)	40
Meat, fish, poultry, 1 ounce (30 g) cooked	7-8
Egg, 1	7
Egg white, 1	3

*4 ounces cooked = size of a deck of cards / 4 ounces cooked = 5 to 6 ounces raw

Plant		Protein (g)
Lentils, beans	1/2 cup (100 g)	7
Baked beans	1/2 cup (130 g)	7
Peanut butter	2 tablespoons (30 g)	8
Tofu	1/4 cake firm (4 ounces, 120 g)	8
Soy milk	1 cup (240 ml)	7

Dairy Products		
Milk, yogurt	1 cup (240 ml)	8
Cheese	1 ounce (30 g)	8
Cheese	1 slice American (2/3 oz; 20 g)	4
Cottage cheese	1/3 cup (75 g)	8
Milk powder	1/4 cup (30 g)	8

Breads, Cereals, Grains		
Bread, 1 slice	(30 g)	2
Cold cereal	1 ounce (30 g)	2
Oatmeal	1/3 cup dry (30 g), or 1 cup cooked	5
Rice	1/3 cup dry (55 g), or 1 cup cooked	4
Pasta	2 ounces dry (60 g), or 1 cup cooked	7

Starchy Vegetables		
Peas, carrots	1/2 cup (80 g) cooked	2
Corn	1/2 cup cooked (80 g)	2
Beets	1/2 cup cooked (80)	2
Winter squash	1/2 cup (100 g)	2
Potato	1 small (125 g)	2

Fruits, Watery Vegetables

Negligible amounts of protein

Most fruits and vegetables have only small amounts of protein. They may contribute a total of 5 to 10 grams of protein per day, depending on how much you eat.

Protein Powders, Shakes and Bars

Soccer players commonly ask Nancy when they should drink a protein shake, and how many protein bars are okay to eat in a day. She then asks them what makes them think they need additional protein. Most hungry players get more than enough protein through standard foods. (Use the sidebar on p. 67 to be sure you are meeting your needs.) Carb deficiency is far more common than protein deficiency! Supplements are not only costly and needless, but also displace bananas, whole grain bagels and other sources of carbs that fuel the muscles.

When you are on the run and grabbing meals, a protein shake or protein bar can be a convenient way to get hassle-free, low-fat protein. But because those are engineered foods, they may lack the wholesome goodness and yet-to-be identified compounds that Nature puts in all natural sources of protein. Most protein bars include protein from whey or casein (milk is about 20% whey, 80% casein), soy and/or egg—all of which are excellent sources of amino acids. Some small bars are handy snacks; others are hefty enough to be a meal replacement. They fall into the category of "convenient" but not "necessary."

"I make sure that I eat protein at dinner——some chicken or steak or something like that. Then, a couple of days before the game, I carbo-load and eat a lot of pasta with a smaller serving of meat."

Lori Chalupny, Midfielder, Saint Louis Athletica

Vegetarian Soccer Players

Some health-conscious soccer players have reduced their meat (and saturated fat) intake, with hopes of reducing their risk of heart disease, or for other health or philosophical reasons. While this can be a good idea, some of these non-meat eaters fail to add any plant proteins to their daily meals. They live on cereal, bagels, pasta, fruit, and vegetables—and they end up with a protein-deficient diet.

While a plant-based diet is good for the environment (factory farming leaves a big carbon footprint), make sure you are addressing your overall protein needs. You need to consume a generous serving of a protein-containing plant food (soy milk, peanut butter, hummus, etc.) at each meal. Otherwise, your performance will suffer from the results of a protein imbalance: chronic fatigue, anemia, lack of improvement, muscle wasting, and an overall run-down feeling.

Beans

For vegetarian soccer players, beans are not only a good source of protein, but also of carbohydrates, B-vitamins (such as folic acid), and fiber. When added to an overall low fat diet, they may help lower elevated blood cholesterol levels. (The problem with beans can be flatulence; some players become gas propelled! If necessary, you can solve this by starting off with small amounts until your system gets used to digesting them.) To add more beans to your sports diet:
- Sauté garlic and onions in a little oil; add canned, drained beans (whole or mashed) and heat together.

Quick and Easy Meatless Meals

Here a few ideas to help you with a meat-free diet that has adequate protein.

Breakfast:

Cold cereal (preferably iron-enriched, as noted on the label):
Top with (soy) milk or yogurt and sprinkled with a few nuts.

Oatmeal, oat bran, and other hot cereals:
Add peanut butter, almonds or other nuts, and/or powdered milk.

Toast, bagels:
Top with low-fat cheese, cottage cheese, or peanut or other nut butters. You can even fortify your nut butters by mixing in powdered skim milk, which does not change the taste.

Snacks:

Assorted nuts
Almond butter on rice cakes or crackers
Yogurt (Note: Frozen yogurt has only 4 grams of protein per cup, as compared to 8 grams of protein in regular yogurt.)

Lunch and Dinner:

Salads:
Add tofu, chick peas (garbanzos), black beans, three-bean salad, kidney beans, cottage or ricotta cheese, sunflower seeds, chopped nuts.

▼

71

Protein-rich salad dressing:

Add salad seasonings to plain yogurt, or blenderized tofu or cottage cheese (diluted with milk or yogurt). Make a tahini (sesame paste) dressing with lemon, salt and other seasonings (try cumin), or add to yogurt for dressing. Delicious!

Spaghetti sauce:

Add diced tofu and/or canned, drained kidney beans. Experiment with the many forms of meat substitutes readily on the market: TVP (textured vegetable protein, a form of soy), crumbled meat substitute in the freezer aisle, canned vegetarian chili with soy, etc.

Pasta:

Choose protein-enriched pastas that offer 13 grams of protein per cup (140 g), as compared to 8 grams in regular pasta. Top with grated part-skim mozzarella cheese.

Potato, sweet potato and yam:

Bake or microwave, then top with canned beans, baked beans, or low-fat cottage or ricotta cheese.

Hearty soups:

Choose lentil, split pea, bean, and minestrone.

Hummus:

Try hummus (garbanzo dip made with tahini) with pita or tortillas.

Cheese pizza:

A protein-rich fast food, half of a 12-inch pizza has about 40 grams of protein.

- Add beans to salads, spaghetti sauce, soups, and stews for a protein booster.
- In a blender, mix black beans, salsa and cheese. Heat in the microwave and use as a dip or on top of tortillas or potatoes.

Try the bean-based recipes in the Recipe Section.

EAT LIKE A BRAZILIAN

Women's Professional Soccer celebrates its share of Brazilian players, among the top in the league and in the world for both men and women. This soccer culture, which plays what is called in Portuguese Juga Bonita (play beautiful, as in: skillfully) has a few typical dishes that lend themselves well to sports performance. Rodízio is a style of eating in both Brazilian and Portuguese restaurants, where food is brought to the tables, usually barbequed meats on a skewer such as sirloin steak or chicken, and distributed in small amounts until the customer has had enough (so it is not a massive piece of meat calling to you from the plate!). Barbequed pineapple or banana serves as a dessert. Rice and beans, a derivitative of Caribbean influence, and a combination that forms a complete protein dish, are also typical Brazilian fare. Try Rosana's Fejioada, a Brazilian classic, featured in the Recipe Section.

Red Meat

Red meats, such as beef and lamb, are indisputably excellent sources of high-quality protein as well as iron (prevents anemia) and zinc (helps with healing). These two minerals are important for optimal health and athletic performance. Yet, some soccer players are a bit unsure if eating red meat is a positive addition to their sports diet. The answer is complex; you need to weigh nutrition facts, ethical concerns, personal values, environmental issues, and dedication to making appropriate food choices. The following information can help you decide if adding two to four servings of red meat into your weekly meals might enhance the quality of your diet.

Meat and cholesterol: Meat, just like chicken, fish, and other animal products, contains cholesterol. Cholesterol is a part of animal cells (but not a part of plant cells). Most animal proteins have similar cholesterol values: 70-80 milligrams of cholesterol per four ounce serving of red meat, poultry, and fish.

Given that the American Heart Association recommends healthy

How to Boost Your Iron Intake

- The recommended intake for iron is 8 milligrams for men and 18 milligrams for women per day. Women have higher iron needs to replace the iron lost from menstrual bleeding. Women who are post-menopausal require only 8 milligrams of iron per day. Young female soccer players should be conscious of their iron intake, as some of them are often found to be low in this mineral, especially the more serious players.
- Iron from animal products is absorbed better than that from plant products.
- A source of vitamin C at each meal enhances iron absorption (such as orange juice or tomato sauce).
- Cooking in cast iron pots also helps increase a food's iron content.

Source		Iron (mg)
Animal Sources (best absorbed)		
Beef, 4 oz	(120 g) cooked	2
Pork, 4 oz	(120 g)	1
Chicken breast, 4 oz	(120 g)	1
Chicken leg, 4 oz	(120 g)	$1^1/_2$
Salmon, 4 oz	(120 g)	1
Fruits		
Prunes, 5	(100 g)	1
Raisins, $^1/_3$ cup	(45 g)	1
Vegetables		
Spinach, $^1/_2$ cup	(100 g) cooked	3
Broccoli, 1 cup	(180 g) cooked	1

▼

Beans		
Kidney, $^1/_2$ cup	(130 g)	$2^1/_2$
Tofu, $^1/_4$ cake	(120 g)	2

Grains		
Cereal, 100% DV iron, 1 oz	(30 g)	18
Spaghetti, 1 cup cooked	(140 g)	2
Bread, 1 oz slice, enriched	(30 g)	1

Other		
Molasses, blackstrap, 1 tablespoon	(15 g)	$3^1/_2$
Wheat germ, $^1/_4$ cup	(30 g)	2

people with normal blood cholesterol levels eat less than 300 milligrams of cholesterol per day, small portions of red meat can certainly fit those requirements. The *saturated* fat in greasy hamburgers, pepperoni, juicy steaks, and sausage are the bigger concern in terms of heart health (and weight). Better choices include London broil, extra-lean hamburger, and top round roast beef. Also, new meats advertising lower fat and other nutritional benefits, such as buffalo, are now beginning to appear in specialty markets and even supermarkets.

Meat and iron: Adequate iron in your sports diet is important to prevent anemia. Without question, the iron in red meat is more easily absorbed than that in popular vegetarian sources of iron (e.g., beans, raisins, spinach) or in supplements. But any iron is better than no iron.

How to Boost Your Zinc Intake

- The recommended intake for zinc is 8 milligrams for women and 11 milligrams for men per day. Young soccer players need zinc to enhance healing and the immune system.
- Animal foods, including seafood, are the best sources of zinc.

Animal Sources		Zinc (mg)
Beef tenderloin, 4 ounces	(120 g)	7
Chicken leg, 4 ounces	(120 g)	3.5
Pork loin, 4 ounces	(120 g)	3
Chicken breast, 4 ounces	(120 g)	1
Cheese, 1 ounce	(30 g)	1
Milk, 1 cup	(240 ml)	1
Oysters, 6 medium, 3 ounces	(90 g)	75 (!)
Tuna, 1 can, 6 ounces	(170 g)	2
Clams, 9 small, 3 ounces	(90 g)	1

Plant Sources		Zinc (mg)
Wheat germ, $1/4$ cup	(30 g)	3.5
Lentils, 1 cup	(200 g)	2.5
Almonds, 1 oz	(30 g)	1
Garbanzo beans, $1/2$ cup	(100 g)	1
Spinach, 1 cup, cooked	(200 g)	0.7
Peanut butter, 1 tablespoon	(15 g)	0.5
Bread, 1 slice, whole wheat	(30 g)	0.5

Meat and zinc: Zinc is important for healing both the minor muscle damage that occurs with daily training as well as major injuries and ailments. It is best found in iron-rich foods (e.g., red meat). Diets deficient in iron may then also be deficient in zinc. Like iron, the zinc in animal products is better absorbed than that in vegetable foods or supplements.

Why Chicken Has Light and Dark Meat

The white and dark meat in chicken (and turkey) is a handy example of the two kinds of muscle fibers that help you exercise:
• Fast-twitch fibers (white breast meat) are used for quick bursts of energy.
• Slow-twitch fibers (dark leg, thigh, and wing meat) function best for endurance exercise.

While soccer is technically not an endurance sport, it can be called a "speed endurance" sport, for which extended and frequent bouts of sprinting are required. This means that most players utilize a combination of both slow-twitch and fast-twitch muscle fibers.

Slow-twitch muscles, more so than fast-twitch, rely on fat for fuel. This is why dark meat contains more fat than the white meat. On the plus side, dark meat also contains more minerals—such as iron, zinc, the same minerals found in red meats.

Chicken, without skin, 4 oz (120 g) cooked	Calories	Fat (g)	Iron (mg)	Zinc (mg)
Breast, white meat	180	4	1.2	1.2
Thigh, dark meat	235	12	1.5	2.7
Leg, dark meat	200	6	1.3	3.6

If you do not eat red meats, you might want to include more dark meat from chicken or turkey in your sports diet. For the small price of a few grams of fat, you'll get more nutritional value. If you want to cut back on fat, eliminate the skin—the fattiest part of poultry.

Get Hooked on Fish

The protein in fish is rich in omega-3 fat, the good fat that protects against heart attacks and strokes. (Even young people are not immune from heart disease. Early signs of heart disease appear in children as young as age 12!) The American Heart Association (AHA) recommends eating two fish meals per week, particularly oily fish, such as trout, salmon, tuna, sardines and herring.

The health benefits of eating fish generally far outweigh the risks—mercury and PCBs (polychlorinated biphenyls). The trick to eating fish is to consume a variety of different types, with a focus on the smaller fish. Each week, enjoy a meal with oily fish (salmon, blue fish) and another with low-mercury fish (pollock, sole). Be moderate, and you'll get hooked on good health.

Youth players often don't tend to choose fish, other than possibly shrimp. If this is the case, try to develop a taste for this healthful food by making "kid friendly" dishes like baked fish and chips (many recipes for this are on the Internet), or try canned salmon sandwiches prepared like tuna (keep in the bones, which are eatable and a good source of calcium).

"Our team often cooks group meals, with everyone contributing a dish. Eating is something we can all do together. We have had a great times sitting around the dinner table and enjoying each other's company. A team that eats together, wins together."

Kendall Fletcher, Midfielder, Saint Louis Athletica

Summary

Protein should be a part of every sports meal—as an accompaniment, not as the main focus. Low-fat milk, yogurt, fish, eggs, poultry and meats are all protein-rich choices, as are beans, nuts, lentils and soy products. While lean red meat is a nutrient-dense sports food, the *fat* in greasy red meats, not the red meat itself, is the primary health culprit. Chicken and fish are lower fat alternatives, with fish being the healthiest choice of all.

If you prefer a vegetarian diet, just be sure to have a protein-rich plant food with each meal. "Vegetarians" who simply eliminate meat and make no effort to include alternate plant sources of protein, iron, and zinc can suffer from dietary deficiencies that hurt their sports performance, and their health. Protein bars can be a handy "emergency food" when you are eating on the run and your protein needs would otherwise be neglected.

Chapter 7
Fats—The Right Kinds for Your Sports Diet

Eat fat, get fat. Eat fat, clog your arteries. Eat fat, have a heart attack. Eat fat, run slow. I'm sure you've heard this anti-fat chatter. While there is an element of truth in some of these statements, there is also room for more education. Let's look at the whole picture.

While dietary fat used to be considered bad, we now know that all fats are not created equal. The hard, saturated fat in beef, butter and cheese is the "bad" fat, as is the trans- (partially hydrogenated) fat that has been in commercially baked goods. The soft, liquid polyunsaturated and monounsaturated fats in fish, olives, peanut butter, and nuts are the "good" fats, essential for fighting inflammation and investing in overall good health. Hence, there's no need to avoid all fat like the plague. You actually should eat a little (health-promoting) fat at each meal to help absorb certain vitamins (A, D, E, K).

Olive oil, the foundation of the acclaimed heart-healthy Mediterranean Diet, is health protective. For centuries, native Italians and Greeks have enjoyed good health and a 40% fat diet (almost double the usual recommended amount). In general, Nancy recommends that healthy soccer players target a sports diet with about 25% of the calories from primarily healthful fat, to allow space in the diet for more carbohydrates.

"For young players, I really recommend packing a lunch. If you go to the food stand at tournaments all they usually have are burgers and fries, and that's not good for you. When you play, the fat just sits. You may think just because you're young you can burn it all off, but unhealthy eating catches up to you in the end."

Danesha Adams, Forward, Chicago Red Stars

How does 25% fat translate into food? Let's say you have 1,800 calories a day in your calorie budget (this would be a reducing diet for most female soccer players):

.25 x 1,800 total calories = 450 calories a day of fat

Because there are 9 calories per gram of fat, divide 450 calories by 9:

450 calories : 9 calories per gram = 50 grams of fat in your daily fat budget

A 25% fat diet includes a reasonable amount and lets you enjoy a little fat at each meal. Preferably, you'll choose fats that have positive health value such as those mentioned in this chapter. But, if you do have the occasional hankering for a big burger with 25 grams of fat and 500 calories, fit it into your day's fat and calorie budget *and balance the rest of the day's meals.* (Refer to Chapter 14 to determine your calorie needs.) Just be aware that with a splurge, all fats are not created equal. A splurge with saturated fatty foods is not the same thing as eating a bowl of guacamole (made from heart-healthy avocado).

"Although I used to eat my fair share of fatty fast food, I now try to eat fish two to three times a week for their health-protective fish oils."

Danesha Adams, Forward, Chicago Red Stars

Fat Guidelines

The following guidelines can help you appropriately budget fat into your food plan.

Calories per day	Fat grams per day (for 25% fat diet)
1,600	45
1,800	50
2,000	55
2,200	60
2,400	65

Fat Content of Some Common Foods

Food			Serving size	Fat (g)	Calories
Dairy products					
Milk,	whole	(3.5% fat)	1 cup (240 ml)	8	150
	reduced-fat	(2% fat)	1 cup (240 ml)	5	120
	low-fat	(1% fat)	1 cup (240 ml)	2	100
	fat-free	(0% fat)	1 cup (240 ml)	--	80
Cheese					
cheddar			1 oz (30 g)	9	110
	reduced-fat		1 oz (30 g)	5	90
mozzarella, part-skim			1 oz (30 g)	5	80
cottage cheese		(4% fat)	1/2 cup (120 g)	5	120
	low-fat	(2% fat)	1/2 cup (120 g)	2	90
cream cheese			1 oz (2 tbsp/30 g)	10	100
	light		1 oz (2 tbsp/30 g)	5	60
ice cream,	gourmet		1/2 cup (100 g)	15	250
	standard		1/2 cup (80 g)	8	150
	light		1/2 cup (70 g)	3	110

Food			Serving size	Fat (g)	Calories
Frozen yogurt,		low-fat	$1/2$ cup (70 g)	2	120
		fat-free	$1/2$ cup (90 g)	--	100
Animal proteins					
Beef,	regular hamburger		4 oz cooked (120 g)	24	330
	flank steak		4 oz cooked (120 g)	12	235
	eye of round		4 oz cooked (120 g)	6	200
Chicken,	breast, no skin		4 oz cooked (120 g)	5	200
	thigh, no skin		4 oz cooked (120 g)	11	235
Fish,	haddock		4 oz cooked (120 g)	1	125
	swordfish		4 oz cooked (120 g)	6	175
Vegetable proteins					
Beans,	kidney		$1/2$ cup cooked (100 g)	--	110
Lentils			$1/2$ cup cooked (100 g)	--	110
Tofu			4 oz (120 g)	5	90
Peanut butter			1 tbsp. (15 g)	8	95
Fats					
Butter			1 tbsp (15 g)	11	100
Margarine			1 tbsp (15 g)	11	100
Oil, olive			1 tbsp (15 g)	13	120
Mayonnaise			1 tbsp (15 g)	11	100
Grains					
Bread,	whole wheat		1 large slice (30 g)	1	90
Crackers,	Saltines		5	2	60
	Ritz		4	4	70
	Rice cakes		1	--	35

Food		Serving size	Fat (g)	Calories
Cereal,	shredded wheat	1 oz ($^2/_3$ cup/ 30 g)	--	90
	granola	1 oz ($^1/_4$ cup/ 30 g)	6	130
	oatmeal	1 oz ($^1/_3$ cup/ 30 g) dry	2	100
Spaghetti, plain		2 oz dry (1 cup cooked; 140 g)	1	210
Rice		2 oz dry (1 cup cooked; 160 g)	--	200
Fast foods				
Big Mac		1	30	560
Egg McMuffin		1	12	300
French fries		small	13	250
KFC fried chicken breast		1	19	380
Pizza, cheese		1 slice large	10-13	250
Snacks, Treats				
Cookie, Chips Ahoy		1 ($^1/_2$ oz; 15 g)	2	50
Fig Newton		1 ($^1/_2$ oz; 15 g)	1	60
Brownie, from mix		1 small	5	140
Graham crackers		2 squares	1	60
Potato chips		1 oz (about 18 chips)	9	150
Pretzels		1 oz (30 g)	1	110
Milky Way		1.75 oz bar (50 g)	8	220
M&Ms w/ peanuts		1.75 oz (50 g) bag	13	250
Reese's Peanut Butter Cups		1.6 oz (2 cups/ 45 g)	15	280
Fruits and Vegetables				
most varieties		negligible fat		

Fear of Fat

Without question, fat imparts a tempting taste, texture, and aroma and helps make food taste great. That's why fatty foods can be hard to resist and are often enjoyed to excess. (Traveling soccer players, in particular, can easily be tempted into eating a high-fat diet.) Although *excess* fat calories can easily turn into body fat, note the "eat fat, get fat" theory is false. Many athletes eat appropriate amounts of fat and stay thin. They simply don't *overeat* calories.

If you obsess about every gram of fat to the extent you have a fat phobia, your fear of fat may be exaggerated. A little fat can actually aid in weight reduction because it takes longer to empty from the stomach—and offers that nice feeling of being satisfied after a meal. For example, you may have less desire to keep munching on, let's say, yet another rice cake if you start by eating a rice cake with a little peanut butter.

As a soccer player, you want to include a little fat in each meal not only to help absorb certain vitamins but also to enhance performance. Runners who boosted their intake of healthful fat from 17% of calories to 30% of calories were not only able to run longer but also had less inflammation afterwards. (Pendergast) Inflammation is what causes muscle fatigue and damage. (Hence, the use of ice, and/or ibuprofen in athletes to bring down inflammation.)

Summary

Soccer players who include some fat in their daily training diet will undoubtedly perform better than those who try to exclude fat. Obviously, choosing more of the *healthful* fats—olive oil, canola oil, nuts, peanut butter, avocado and salmon—is preferable to loading up on the fat from buttery cookies, greasy burgers, and gourmet ice cream. But all fats eaten in moderation can be balanced into an overall healthful sports diet.

Chapter 8
Fluids, Water and Sports Drinks

Dehydration is one of the major causes of fatigue while playing soccer. Hence preventing dehydration is a vital part of your sports diet. While recreational soccer players are unlikely to become dehydrated if they are practicing for an hour or less of low-key soccer in cool weather, serious soccer players with sweat-soaked uniforms want to be sure to drink adequate fluids, not only in hot weather, but also in cool weather when they may not think to drink. They might be losing two to three quarts (liters) per match, if not more. And on typical tournament weekends, that really adds up.

Younger soccer players are also at risk for becoming dehydrated. Children have less capacity for sweating, and their body temperature can rise quickly if they become dehydrated. If you are the coach or parent of a young soccer player, be sure to provide frequent fluid breaks, preferably in the shade. If the soccer field does not offer shade, consider requesting that the team invest in a portable open-sided tent with a roof to set up along the sidelines during the game for at least a little shade.

While you don't have to replace every drop of sweat, your goal should be to limit sweat loss to 2% of your body weight (Montain). That is:

If you weigh:	Do not lose more than:
100 lbs (45 kg)	2 lbs (1 kg)
125 lbs (57 kg)	2.5 lbs (1.2 kg)
150 lbs (68 kg)	3 lbs (1.5 kg)

Your heart rate increases by 3 to 5 beats per minute for every one percent of body weight loss. Hence, with increasing sweat losses, exercise feels harder; you'll enjoy it less, and you'll move slower. In extreme cases, becoming dehydrated can contribute to medical problems.

When you are training hard day after day in the heat—perhaps doing double sessions pre-season or playing multi-game tournaments—you can easily become chronically dehydrated. You'll feel unusually fatigued and lethargic. Don't let that happen!

You can tell if you are well-hydrated by monitoring your urine:
- You should urinate frequently (every 2 to 4 hours) throughout the day. (Check with your players on game or tournament days.)
- The urine should be clear and of significant quantity.
- Your morning urine should *not* be dark and concentrated. (See the Urine Color Chart.)

"The biggest nutrition improvement I've made since coming to Women's Professional Soccer is drinking more water. Drinking enough has made a significant impact on my energy level and performance on the field."

Lisa De Vanna, Forward,
Washington Freedom

Thirst is a clear signal your body needs fluids. You want to drink *before* you feel thirsty. Or, you can follow the advice of the American College of Sports Medicine and learn your sweat rate so you can drink the right amount to match your sweat losses.

To determine how much you should drink during exercise, weigh yourself (without clothes) before and after a soccer game. Keep track of how much you drink; 16 ounces of water (or sports drink) weighs one pound. If you drank nothing and lost two pounds (32 ounces or 1 quart or about 1 liter) in 60 minutes, you should plan to drink accordingly during the next exercise session— at least 8 ounces (225 ml) for every fifteen minutes of physical activity. If you struggle with muscle cramps (often associated with dehydration), you might want to monitor your weight, to see if you are keeping up with your fluid needs.

If you weigh 120 pounds (55 kg), try not to lose more than $2^{1}/_{2}$ pounds (1 kg) of sweat during a workout. Practice drinking fluids during training as a means to teach your stomach to comfortably accommodate the liquid. Your body can turn water into sweat in about 10 minutes, so keep drinking, even towards the end of practice sessions or, if possible, games.

Urine Color Chart

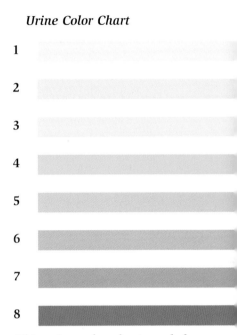

This urine color chart can help you determine if you have been consuming enough fluids to stay well-hydrated. If your urine is darker than 3, drink more!

Courtesy of Lawrence Armstrong, PhD, Universiy of Connecticut

WHY THE HEADACHES?

Young players often complain of headaches. Frequently, the cause is dehydration, but without realizing this, many simply take significant amounts of ibuprofen (such as Advil) to address the problem. At one clinic, a soccer parent mentioned to Gloria that she too had headaches. As a follow up, more water worked for her (turns out even watching games in the heat can bring on dehydration!), as it does for many players. Also, watch over-consumption of ibuprofen (taken for a variety of reasons), which can be common in the youth soccer community. In addition to causing physical problems (especially if taken on an empty stomach), this medication can mask the signs of injury, potentially causing only further damage.

Playing Soccer in the Heat

When playing soccer in the heat, pay attention to your teammates and also listen to your own body. If you notice that you or your teammates feel light-headed, dizzy, nauseous, clumsy, uncoordinated, confused, irrational, have stopped sweating, or have ashen gray pale skin, stop playing immediately! These are all symptoms of heat illness.

Here's what to do:
• lay down in a shady or cool place.
• raise legs and hips to improve blood pressure.
• remove excess clothing.
• cool off by wetting the skin liberally and fanning vigorously.
• apply ice pack to groin, armpits and neck.
• drink cool water.

Better yet, try to avoid heat illness. Acclimate yourself to heat by starting off gradually in your intensity level and playing time for a couple of weeks, if possible. If heat is sudden (such as traveling to a tournament or a sudden change in weather), take extra care to hydrate well and play sensibly. Coaches should attempt to make liberal use of subs, and be on the lookout for signs of heat exhaustion.

"I drink water throughout the day. I try to always have a bottle or glass of water with me wherever I am, so it is always available. When I drink too little, I tend to cramp up."

(A cramping phenomenon expressed by numerous Women's Professional Soccer and other players.) Nicole Barnhart, Goalkeeper, FC Gold Pride

Water or Sports Drinks?

Water is an adequate fluid replacer during soccer sessions that last less than 60 minutes, particularly if you have fueled-up with a pre-exercise snack. Sports drinks are helpful during training sessions and games that last longer than 60 to 90 minutes or on multiple game days; they replace both water and some carbohydrates. Because carbs help maintain a normal blood sugar level needed to feed your brain, you'll discover you'll perform better, think clearer, make better decisions, and feel better after playing.

For youth soccer (or any age soccer, for that matter), orange sections + water, watermelon, pretzels + water are all options that will refresh players between halves and offer more nutritional value than a sports drink. Sports drinks are essentially sugar water with a dash of salt. A sports drink provides:
- small amounts of *carbohydrates* to fuel your mind and muscles.
- *sodium* to enhance water absorption and retention.
- *water* to replace sweat losses.

Sports drinks are designed to be consumed *during* exercise that lasts longer than an hour. However, soccer sells a lot of sports drinks. They seem to be a staple at every game and practice, yet there is no need to drink them throughout the day. A constant intake can damage your teeth, so limit them to playing. With the multitude of sports drinks on the market, you may feel confused about what's best to drink, and wonder if some are better than the others. The bottom line is that you should choose the drink that tastes best to you; there are no significant advantages to one over the other. The most important point is to *drink enough.* (For more specific information, see Chapter 11.)

SPORTS DRINK TIPS

If your team spends a fortune on Gatorade or other sports drinks (a staple of youth soccer), consider investing in the much less expensive and easier to carry sports drink powder, which is reconstituted with water. Purchase a large thermal cooler, and mix up a big team batch with ice pre-game. Bring disposable cups. This guarantees every player can equally rehydrate.

If the players are casual exercisers and do not need to replace calories, plain water is just fine. Or, use individual player drink bottles and dilute the sports drink with water or ice. You can also make sports drink ice cubes to melt in water-filled bottles, just to flavor the water.

Comparing Common Fluid Replacers

Beverage (8 oz)	Calories	Sodium (mg)	Potassium (mg)
Propel	10	35	0
Gatorade	50	110	30
Gatorade Endurance	50	200	90
PowerAde	70	55	30
Cola	100	5	--
Beer	100	12	60
Orange juice	110	2	475
Cranapple juice	175	5	70
Fruit yogurt	250	150	465
Possible losses in 2 hours	1,000	1,000	180

Sodium Replacement

When you sweat, you lose sodium, an electrolyte (electrically charged particle) that helps maintain proper water balance in your tissues. Most recreational soccer players don't have to worry about replacing sodium during exercise because the losses are generally too small to cause a deficit that will impair performance and/or health.

But, if you will be playing for more than three or four hours (such as pre-season or soccer camp) or are a salty sweater (as noted by salt stains on your skin and clothing), sodium loss can become problematic. Be sure to consume more than plain water during that time; choose sports drinks *and* foods that contain sodium. Consuming endurance sports drinks (with more sodium than the standard sports drink), pretzels, V-8 juice, chicken broth, salt packets (from a restaurant), pickles and adding more salt to other foods are just a few ways to boost sodium intake.

Drinking *excessive* plain water dilutes the sodium outside the cells. This causes too much water to seep into cells and the cells swell—including the cells in the brain—potentially causing hyponatremia (low blood sodium). Symptoms of this that progressively appear include feeling weak, groggy, nauseous, incoherent, and ultimately stumbling, seizures, coma, and death.

Sodium in Commonly Eaten Foods

In general, most novice players consume adequate sodium, even without adding salt to their food. But, if you crave salt, you should eat it. Salt cravings signal that your body wants salt. If you hanker for some pretzels or salty foods after a long game, eat them!

Here are some common sources of sodium that can easily replace the estimated 500 milligrams of sodium you might lose in an hour of soccer.

Food	Sodium (mg)
Bread, 1 slice	150
Cheese, 1 oz (30 g)	220
Egg, 1	60
Yogurt, 8 oz/240 ml	125
Broth, canned 8 oz/240 ml	900
Pizza, 2 slices	1,200
Whopper	1,450

The rule of thumb is to add extra salt to your diet if you have lost more than 4 to 6 pounds of sweat (3 to 4% of your body weight pre- to post-exercise). Salty sweaters (who end up with a crust of salt on their skin after a hard game) and heavy sweaters (who lose more than 2 lbs sweat per hour, characterized by soaked clothing) should pay close attention to their sodium intake—particularly if they are not acclimatized to exercising in the heat. (See Chapter 9 for more information on good products for sodium replacement.)

"When you are playing soccer in the heat, you have to make sure that you're not only drinking enough fluids but also eating enough calories. That's the one problem I've run into as far as my nutrition."

Lori Chalupny, Midfielder, Saint Louis Athletica

How to Keep Your Cool

Here's a short true-false quiz to test your knowledge about fluid replacement and help you survive the heat in good health and with high energy.

True or False: *Drinking cold water during practices and games will cool you off.* **True** (but by a small margin). Although drinking cold water will cool you off slightly more than warmer water, the difference is small. That's because the water quickly warms to body temperature.

The more important concern is drinking enough quantity of fluid. Any fluid of any temperature is better than no fluid. Because cold fluids tend to be more palatable than warm fluids, they tend to be the more popular option. For hot weather, when fluids left on the bench quickly become warm, consider bringing a cooler as a way to keep a supply of cool beverages on hand. Or, use a large amount of ice, or freeze drinks first and drink them as they thaw, and/or invest in a thermal water bottle or covering.

STAYING HYDRATED WHILE PLAYING

Unless the conditions are so harsh that game or tournament organizers arrange special water breaks, soccer does not traditionally include breaks other than half-time or injury time. However, there is no ironclad rule that prohibits a team from placing bottles conveniently located outside the side or end lines, or receiving them from parents or fans (as long as those spectators do not cross the line onto the field) during brief breaks in play (such as injury time). Most players and families do not take advantage of this opportunity, often because they simply don't realize they can, or don't see others doing it. While the referee may stop you if he/she deems this hydration tactic interferes with the game, why not check with officials before playing to ask about their policy. It could save your game, and your health.

True or False: *Bottled water is a soccer necessity.*
False. Players and their families drink a lot of bottled water. They may think it is safer and healthier. They spend a lot of money buying it, struggle to lug it, and often end up with the small bottles, which are not nearly enough for even one game or practice.

The Environmental Protection Agency has higher standards for tap water than the FDA has for bottled, and one-fourth of all bottled water is repackaged tap water. Tap water is safe, cheaper and more environmentally friendly than bottled. So let your tap water run for a minute to get any possible lead or other residue out of the pipes, and fill your water bottles.

True or False: *Dieters should pay attention to liquid calories.*
True. The calories you drink are more likely to contribute to fat gain than calories you chew. That's because liquid calories are less filling and don't contribute much to satiety (that satisfying feeling of having been fed). Think of a regular soda as a sugary treat, not as a thirst quencher. But think of (low-fat chocolate) milk as a satiating "liquid food" that offers carbs, protein and sodium. It's the recovery beverage of champions, and has been instituted as the immediate post-game beverage in many soccer and sports programs in the nation.

Summary

Soccer players who fail to drink enough fluids on a daily basis will suffer from chronic fatigue. If they fail to drink enough during a game, they will be unable to perform at their best, and can potentially develop serious medical problems. Your best bet is to *prevent* dehydration by drinking enough fluids throughout the day, so that you need to urinate every two to hour hours and your urine is pale colored. While drinking a sports drink during a game can be a smart choice, at other times you want to enjoy water, juice, low-fat milk, and watery foods like melon and berries. You need not drink plain water, per se, to meet your fluid needs. The standard diet provides more than enough electrolytes (sodium), but if you crave salt or are a salty sweater, you should likely eat some salty foods.

Chapter 9
Engineered Sports Foods:
Convenience or Necessity?

To look at all the ads for sports drinks, energy bars, electrolyte replacers, and sports candies, you'd think these engineered products are a necessary part of a sports diet. Soccer players routinely ask Nancy for advice about how to use these products. Before she can answer their questions about which (if any) commercial sports foods are valuable for enhancing performance, she first needs to assess their daily sports diet to determine if they can get—or are getting—what they need from standard foods.

Many soccer athletes believe commercial sports foods are the best sources of carbohydrates and sodium. Wrong. In most cases, a wisely chosen sports diet can supply all their needs—plus more!

While there is a time and a place for engineered sports foods (particularly among players who train at high intensity), many players and their families needlessly waste a lot of money misusing them. The purpose of this chapter is to help you become an informed consumer, so you can understand how best to use these products, and wisely spend your soccer dollars.

Pre-exercise Energy Bars

Fueling with a pre-workout energy bar and sports drink is an expensive way ($2 to $3) to energize your workout. You could less expensively consume 300 calories of banana+yogurt+water ($1) or pretzels+raisins+water (50¢). These choices, or ones like them, are carbohydrate-rich and will offer the fuel your muscles need for a stellar workout. Commercial energy bars do not contain any magic ingredients that will enhance performance more than, for example, a granola bar, bagel, or fig cookies and water. Standard supermarket foods can do that as well as engineered foods.

The best pre-soccer snacks digest easily, settle well in your stomach, and do not "talk back to you." Experiment to determine what foods your body accommodates best. (Refer to Chapter 10 for more information about how to fuel best before exercise.)

Energy Drinks

Energy drinks offer enough sugar and caffeine to give most any athlete a quick energy boost. The problem is, one quick fix will not compensate for missed meals. That is, if you sleep through breakfast and barely eat lunch, having a Red Bull for a pre-workout energizer will unlikely compensate for the previous inadequate food intake. If you can make the time to train, you can also make the time to fuel appropriately, rather than rely on a quick fix.

Caffeine

A popular "ergogenic aid," caffeine enhances performance by making the effort seem easier. For players who are accustomed to consuming caffeine, a pre-exercise caffeine-fix—especially if accompanied by carbs (e.g. from food)—can energize your workout. But for other players, caffeine can make them feel nervous, jittery, and nauseous. Be sure to experiment with pre-exercise caffeine during training to determine how your body responds. For some, an effective intake is about 1.5 mg caffeine per pound of body weight (3 mg/kg), or about 200 mg for a 150 pound player, but tolerance varies greatly.

Here's how the options compare:

Option	Caffeine (mg)	Cost
Coca-Cola, 20 oz	60	$1.59
Red Bull, 8 oz	80	$2.19
Nodoz, 1 tablet	200	$0.33
Coffee, home brew, 16 oz	200	$0.20
Starbuck's, 16 oz	300	$1.94

At one time, caffeine was thought to have a dehydrating effect, but we now know that is not true. Research suggests caffeine does not contribute to excessive water loss and is okay to consume, even in the heat. (Armstong 2002, 2005).

"Recently, I've preferred to drink caffeine drinks before games. Sometimes I'll even have GU (gel) with caffeine to give myself a little boost of energy, making me feel more alert and ready to play. It's not traditional in my native England, but with new information, these products are becoming a lot more common in competitive sports across the board."

Anita Asante, Defender, Sky Blue FC

Sports Drinks

Many athletes believe the sodium in sports drinks is essential to replace the sodium lost in sweat. Wrong. Sports drinks are actually relatively low in sodium compared to what you consume in your meals. Sodium enhances fluid retention and helps keep you better hydrated, as compared to plain water.

If you sweat heavily, you might lose about 1,000 to 3,000 mg sodium in an hour of hard exercise. Here are options for replacing these sodium losses:

Replacements	Sodium (mg)
Endurolytes, 1 capsule	40
PowerBar Electrolytes, 8 oz	65
Gatorade, 8 oz	110
Gatorade Endurance, 8 oz	200
Cheese stick, 1 oz	200
Pizza, 1 slice	500
Salt, $1/4$ teaspoon	600
Soup, 1 can Campbell's	2,200

As you can see, in terms of sodium, there is no need for any soccer player to consume a sports drink with her lunch, because the soup or cheese sandwich have far more sodium than the small amount of sodium in the sports drink. By consuming some salty food such as 8 ounces of chicken broth before exercising in the heat, you can get a hefty dose of sodium into your body before you even begin to play. Having salty pre-exercise food has also been shown to enhance endurance. (Sims)
(If soup isn't for you, have other equivalents, such as salted baked chips.)

Electrolytes

One collegiate soccer player reported using electrolyte drinks throughout the day. He then admitted he didn't even know what electrolytes are. They are electrically charged particles, more commonly known as sodium, calcium, magnesium, and potassium. Standard foods abound with electrolytes, more so than engineered sports foods. Note how few electrolytes the engineered foods contain compared to real foods.

	Sodium (mg)	Calcium (mg)	Magnesium (mg)	Potassium (mg)
Endurolytes (1 capsule)	40	50	25	25
Nuun, 1 tab	360	12	25	100
PBJ & milk	600	300	130	750
Pizza, 1 slice	650	200	30	220

Vitamin Water and Vitamin-Enriched Sports Foods

Many engineered foods tout they are enriched with B-vitamins "for energy." True, B-vitamins are needed to convert food into energy, but they are not sources of energy. The body has a supply of vitamins stored in the liver, so you are unlikely to become deficient during exercise.

Soccer players—who eat far more food, hence more vitamins, than do sedentary people—have the opportunity to consume abundant vitamins. A large bowl of Wheaties offers 100% of the Daily Value (DV) for B-vitamins. (Most cereals, breads, pastas and other grain foods are enriched with B-vitamins, unless they are "all natural.") Eight ounces of orange juice offers 100% of the DV for Vitamin C. In contrast, 8 ounces of Energy Tropical Citrus Vitamin Water offers only 40% of the DV for C. Check labels on all these products to comparison shop.

"I believe the saying: 'You are what you eat.' In order for your body to be able to perform to its full potential, you need to be putting the right things into it, so you have the energy you need and your body has the vitamins and nutrients it needs to maintain and repair itself, and recover from workouts."

Nicole Barnhart, Goalkeeper, FC Gold Pride

Sports Gels and Sports Candy

During intense games, consuming a gel or sports drink at half time can help boost your energy. So can any sugary food—honey, jelly beans, sports beans, defizzed cola. Think twice before you spend your money on Sports Beans ($1/100-calorie packet) for an afternoon snack. Like sports drinks, sports beans are designed to be consumed during exercise. Regular jelly beans would be a far less expensive snack. Better yet, raisins, dried pineapple, or grapes are a healthier snack option.

Summary

Not everyone needs sports foods to enhance their performance. While they can be a convenient source of pre-wrapped calories that travel well, they are not magic. Many soccer players report standard foods taste better and are more enjoyable. As an educated consumer, learn what works best for your body. And always *experiment first during training* with any new food or fuel that you might use during a game!

SECTION III

SPORTS NUTRITION—
EATING TO WIN

Chapter 10
Fueling Before Practices and Games

One of the biggest mistakes made by soccer players—particularly those who rush from school to practice or from work to workout—is to train on empty. They report they have "no time" to eat. Our response is: If you have time to be on a team, you have time to fuel for both training and competition. Be responsible!

- If you are training on empty because you want to shed a few pounds of undesired body fat, think again. While losing excess flab can indeed help the overweight soccer player to run faster, attempting to lose the weight during training sessions or games contributes to needless fatigue while playing. You can lose weight at other times of the day, but you shouldn't attempt to play soccer on fumes! Just as your car works best with gas in its tank, your body works best when it has been appropriately fueled. (For detailed weight reduction information, please read Chapter 16.)

- If you have always abstained from eating within the hour or two before you play just because you think you should exercise with an empty stomach, think again. Pre-soccer food actually contributes to greater stamina and endurance. We encourage you to *try* 100 to 300 calories of a light snack (e.g. crackers, banana, toast). You might be pleasantly surprised by the benefits—more energy, better concentration and focus, greater stamina, and better ability to keep up with the opponent at the end of the game.

- If you avoid pre-exercise eating because it contributes to intestinal distress, start training your intestinal tract to tolerate food. If pre-exercise food jostles in your stomach, and either "talks back" or stimulates the urge to have a bowel movement, you'll want to train your intestinal track to tolerate small amounts of pre-exercise food—a saltine, a pretzel—and gradually increase to 100 to 300 calories of a pre-soccer snack.

Because eating ability and food preferences vary in relation to when, how long, and how hard you train, all players who plan to build up to more than an hour of soccer should *practice* pre-exercise eating. Remember, you are training your intestinal track, as well as your heart, lungs and muscles.
Experiment with the following pre-exercise eating recommendations so you can learn through trial and error:

- what foods work best for your body
- when you should eat them
- what amounts are appropriate

You are an experiment of one, and only *you* can ultimately determine what works best for your body.

"I like to make sure I get a good, solid, well-balanced meal about 3-4 hours prior to the game. Just prior to leaving for the game or in the locker room, I am a big fan of eating fruit (bananas and apples) with peanut butter, or I pack a peanut butter and jelly sandwich to take with me. "

Nicole Barnhart, Goalkeeper, FC Gold Pride

Soccer involves short, intense bursts of exercise. The harder you play, the less likely you will want too much pre-exercise fuel and the more likely you will need to allow more digestion time between eating and playing. Some players may feel nauseated at even the thought of pre-exercise food, while youth players may appreciate the added energy. In general, if you are exercising at a pace you can comfortably maintain for more than 30 minutes (jogging, easy practice sessions), you can both exercise and digest food at the same time. At this comfortable training pace, the blood flow to the stomach is 60 to 70% of normal— adequate to maintain normal digestion processes.

During intense sprinting, the stomach essentially shuts down and gets only about 20% of its normal blood flow. Then, when the exercise becomes less intense, digestion resumes. Hence, soccer players can digest and utilize pre-exercise fuel during stop-and-start exercise. The limiting factor is individual tolerance. If pre-exercise fuel feels uncomfortable and causes indigestion or heartburn, you'll want to allow extra digestion time prior to a hard workout. Or, select sports gels and foods and fluids designed to be eaten during strenuous exercise.

Five Benefits of Pre-Soccer Fueling

If you are in the experimental stage of developing your pre-soccer food plan for various intensities of practices and drills, the following information provides some helpful facts about the benefits of proper fueling. This information can help you find the right combination of food and fluids that will make or break your ability to train and compete comfortably.

1. Pre-soccer food helps prevent low blood sugar.
The carbohydrates in your pre-exercise bagel, oatmeal, banana, yogurt or other carb-based snack are important because they fuel not only your muscles but also your mind. Adequate pre-soccer carbohydrates help you think clearly; the carbs digest into sugar and travel via the bloodstream to provide fuel for your brain. Why suffer with light-headedness, needless fatigue, irritability, and inability to concentrate when you can prevent these symptoms of low blood sugar (hypoglycemia)?

Carbs that you eat several hours pre-exercise, such as the pasta lunch before an afternoon game or the oatmeal-with-raisins breakfast, get stored in not only your muscles but also your liver. They are released into the blood stream as needed to maintain a normal blood sugar level. Overnight, the blood sugar levels drop as the liver glycogen stores get low. That's why fueling with cereal or a bagel before a morning practice or game is important; it feeds your brain.

Low blood sugar also happens in the afternoon if you fail to eat enough breakfast and lunch. You will feel tired, unable to concentrate on the task at hand, and perform poorly. This is needless and preventable. Enjoying a pre-soccer snack such as a granola bar, banana or a half a sandwich, or eating more heartily at breakfast and lunch will help you have enough energy to get through the afternoon soccer session.

Soccer players often participate in morning games without having first eaten, or having eaten poorly. Some report they feel fine and enjoy good energy. That might be because they ate a big dinner the night before and/or did some serious late-night snacking that bolstered their liver glycogen stores and reduced their need for a morning energizer. This pattern is not bad or wrong, as long as it works well for them. (In general, athletes who eat heavily at the end of the day tend to have more body fat than those who fuel evenly during the day.)

STAY IN THE GAME

Some statistics reveal that the majority of goals are scored in the last five minutes of the first and second half of the game. And according to an analysis of goals scored at the 2002 men's World Cup, the peak of scoring was between the 76th and 90th minutes of the matches. That means that most likely, fatigue and/or lack of focus has a major impact on allowing opponents to score. This is most apparent on the youth soccer level. Smart nutrition can keep you in the game, and competitive until the final whistle.

Analysis by W.W.S. Njororai, African Journal for Physical, Health Education, Recreation and Dance.

2. Pre-soccer food abates hunger feelings, absorbs some of the gastric juices, and for some players, helps settle the stomach.
A little snack (toast, pretzels, graham crackers) helps some soccer players feel better. They can exercise comfortably soon after snacking on a few crackers or a piece of fruit—but may prefer to wait three or four hours after a heartier meal. The caloric density of the snack or meal affects the rate at which the food leaves the stomach. Hence, the general "rule of thumb" before a hard practice or game is to allow:

- 3-4 hours for a large meal to digest
- 2-3 hours for a smaller meal
- 1-2 hours for a blended or liquid meal
- less than an hour for a small snack, as tolerated

3. Pre-soccer carbohydrates fuel the muscles.
The snack you eat even within the hour before you play can get digested into glucose and burned for energy. If you have trouble with solid foods (i.e., banana, bagel) before you play, you might want to experiment with liquids, such as a fruit smoothie, low-fat yogurt, or a canned liquid meal such as Boost.

In general, carbohydrate-based snacks are digested more easily than fatty foods. Low-fat foods and meals tend to digest easily and settle well. In comparison, high-fat-bacon-and-fried-egg breakfasts, greasy hamburgers, tuna subs loaded with mayonnaise, and grilled cheese sandwiches have been known to settle heavily and feel uncomfortable. Too much fat slows digestion, so the meal lingers longer in the stomach and may contribute to a weighed-down feeling. A little fat, however, such as in a slice of low-fat cheese on toast, a skimming of peanut butter on a bagel, or the fat in some brands of energy bars, can be appropriate. It provides both sustained energy and satiety for the long run.

EASIER SAID THAN DONE

Young players often "forget to eat," or push away offers of food, saying they aren't hungry. This is usually due to distraction, initial loss of appetite from exertion, or nervous excitement due to the competition (or even try-outs). Gloria's experience is that when teams, or groups of players, eat together, this situation changes. Players relax, find their appetites, and discover enjoyment and purpose in fueling themselves. What's more, there is an added competitive edge when teammates realize they are going the extra mile to increase their game preparation. (And other players in the area see their competition meaningfully fueling their bodies, and recognize their opponents are purposefully preparing to compete.)

Pre-Soccer Meal and Snack Suggestions

Here are some popular high-carbohydrate pre-soccer meal suggestions that keep your muscles well fueled. Be sure to experiment during training to determine the correct portion for your body that settles well:

Breakfast:	cold cereals, oatmeal and other hot cereals, bagels, English muffins, pancakes, French toast with syrup, jam, honey, fruit, juice
Lunch:	sandwiches (with the bread being the "meat " of the sandwich), fruit, thick-crust pizza, hearty broth-based soups with noodles or rice
Dinner:	pasta, potato, or rice entrées; veggies, breads, juice, fruit
Snacks:	flavored yogurt, pretzels, crackers, fig bars, frozen yogurt, dry cereal, leftover pasta, zwieback, energy bars, simple biscuit-type cookies, animal crackers, canned and fresh fruits, juice

4. *Pre-soccer beverages provide fluids to fully hydrate your body.* By drinking diluted juice or sports drinks before you exercise, you can optimize your fluid intake, as well as boost your carbohydrate and energy intake. The best pre-exercise fluid choices include water, sports drinks, diluted juices, hot chocolate and even coffee or tea if you want a caffeine-boost. Despite popular belief, caffeine is not dehydrating. It is known to be energizing and to make the effort seem easier—particularly if older players are accustomed to drinking coffee or tea (and are unlikely to get "the jitters" or suffer from "coffee stomach").

5. *Pre-soccer food can pacify your mind with the knowledge that your body is well fueled.*

Pre-soccer food has great psychological value. If you firmly believe that a specific food (such as a bagel with peanut butter) will enhance your performance, then it probably will. Your mind has power over your body's ability to perform at its best. If you do have a "magic food" that assures athletic excellence, you should make sure that food or meal is available prior to every game!

"When we have an evening game, I eat a big breakfast, a lighter lunch, and then I make sure I don't go too crazy with food before the game. It's difficult to work out really hard on a full stomach."

Amy Rodriguez, Forward, Philadelphia Independence

Summary

Whether you are a novice or competitive soccer player, pre-exercise food will help you better enjoy your soccer program. Just as you put gas in your car before you take it for a drive, you should put 100 to 300 calories of carbohydrate-rich food in your body within the hour before you play. You may need to train your intestinal track to tolerate this fuel, just like you train your heart, lungs and muscles to go the distance. Granted, each player is an experiment of one, and some players can tolerate food better than others. That's why you need to experiment *during training* to determine what pre-exercise menu works best for you.

Chapter 11
Foods and Fluids During Practices and Games

Once you start training or playing games that last for more than 60 to 90 minutes, you should try hard to consume fuel *during* the session. The same would be true if you haven't eaten a sufficient pre-game meal, have back-to-back games, or are a young player who could benefit from more energy.

Professional women soccer players may burn 1,000 calories a game, and men, 1,500. Hence, learning how to fuel during intense games can help delay fatigue and dehydration. If you are a coach, be sure to encourage your players to drink whenever possible—including during breaks in play and at halftime.

More precisely, your goals during soccer practices and games are to:

1)   drink the right amount of fluid to prevent dehydration—and overhydration.
2)   consume enough carbs to prevent hypoglycemia (low blood sugar).

You can succeed at meeting these goals by drinking carbohydrate-containing fluids (such as a sports drink) or by combining water with solid foods (orange slices; watermelon; water + energy bar; water + sports gels). You'll rarely see elite soccer players consuming more than a sports drink during the game, but youth soccer players can do well with a variety of fluids and foods, especially at halftime.

"I sometimes cramp during games, so I work hard to stay well hydrated and well fueled. I always drink lots of water and a sports drink before I play. At halftime, I sometimes have a few bites of an energy bar."

Rachel Buehler, Defender, FC Gold Pride

Creating a Fueling Plan

During training sessions, be sure to drink every 15 to 20 minutes. Remember, you want to *prevent* dehydration. Don't let yourself get too thirsty. By drinking on a schedule—let's say, a target of about 4-8 ounces (120-240 ml), that's 4-8 gulps, of water or sports drink every 15 to 20 minutes—you can minimize dehydration, maximize your performance, and reduce your recovery time. As explained in Chapter 8, learning your sweat rate helps you determine how much to drink and is important information, particularly if you sweat heavily. Be certain you make the effort to weigh yourself before and after a one-hour soccer session so you'll know how much sweat you lose (and need to replace); one pound sweat = one pound of water lost (16 ounces; 480 g). Also, if possible in hot weather games, place water along the sidelines to be consumed during breaks in play.

Within the first half-hour of playing soccer, start drinking so you can maintain adequate hydration; once you are dehydrated, you won't catch up. Losing only 2% of your body weight (2.5 pounds for a 125-pound player; 1.1 kg for a 57 kg player) from sweating hurts your performance and upsets your ability to regulate your body temperature. (Refer to Chapter 8 for more details.) To keep hydrated, bring one or two bottles of sports drinks and a bottle of water. Bringing extra fluids is always safer than being stuck with too little fluid. However, since it is rare to be able to drink extensively during a game, "tank up" as much as possible, but without feeling uncomfortable sloshing in the stomach or that you have to urinate. Experiment in training first.

In training, you should drink according to a schedule, but you should also pay attention to thirst. Don't force fluids. Drinking too much fluid to the point you feel the excess water sloshing around in your stomach can make you feel nauseous. The immediate solution is to stop drinking for a while. The long-term solution is to practice drinking during training sessions, so you can learn the appropriate fluid intake.

"I normally enjoy some sports drink before a game. At halftime, I have more sports drink and some kind of gel or other carb to keep my blood sugar from dropping. I lose so much energy in the first half."

Cat Whitehill, Defender, Washington Freedom

You will feel in a better mood and more energetic if you can replace not only water but also carbohydrates. These carbohydrates help to maintain a normal blood sugar level as well as provide a source of energy for muscles—and help you avoid hitting "the wall." The carbs you consume will also help keep you in good spirits. Some poorly-fueled soccer players become moody, irritable, and irrational towards the end of a long soccer session. They lose focus, play "flat," and/or get overly frustrated with their mistakes, resulting in poor performance.

THE PHYSICAL NEEDS OF THE GAME

Soccer is a game of constant motion. In addition to being physically fit, consider how much "premium fuel" it takes to play well in terms of nutrition.

For the older player (but a good overview for players at all ages and levels):
- 5 to 6.5 miles covered per game (2.5 for goalkeepers)
- 1,000 activity changes per game, meaning a change of speed or direction every 6 seconds
- Games are typically played at 75% of a person's physical limits
- Rest pauses happen for about 3 seconds every 2 minutes

U.S. Soccer Sports Medicine book, compiled by Performance Conditioning for Soccer Newsletter.

Fuel Suggestions

Some suggestions for fueling during a long practice or game include sports drink, watermelon, orange sections, and gels. Whereas the more serious soccer players are able to do well with just a sports drink, novice players might enjoy some fruit or watery food. There is no magic to the special sports foods (e.g. gels, sports beans, energy bars) you see advertised. These engineered foods are simply pre-wrapped and convenient. Use them if you prefer, but also know you could save money by eating raisins and bananas (e.g. 3 fig bar cookies equal the same nutritional value in a Powerbar). (See Chapter 9 for more information.)

Popular Snacks During a Long Soccer Practice or Game

A plethora of commercial sports snacks are available for fueling during exercise that lasts longer than 60 to 90 minutes. Yet "real foods" can work just as well. Experiment with a variety of flavors (sweet, sour, salty), knowing that tastes change as you become fatigued.

Young players and professional players alike benefit greatly from at least halftime refueling. This is particularly true if the pre-game meal has been a small one.

Sports drinks

Sports gels or Sports beans

Water with banana

Watermelon

Grapes

Orange slices

Summary

Preventing dehydration and low blood sugar is crucial to being able not only to survive but also to be successful in extended or intense soccer playing. The fluids and foods that you consume during training or games should be an extension of your carbohydrate-rich daily training diet. Because each player has individual tolerances and preferences, you want to learn by trial and error during training what foods and fluids settle best and contribute to top competitive performance.

Chapter 12
Recovery After Intense Practices and Games

Novice or recreational soccer players are unlikely to exhaust themselves during hour-long workouts, or deplete their muscles of glycogen, or become dehydrated. They need not worry about rapidly refueling their bodies. Although they do need to develop good eating habits for future more serious play, and so benefit by understanding this aspect of sports nutrition. Serious soccer players, in comparison, can end up depleted, exhausted and dehydrated during intense exercise that lasts longer than an hour. They need to carefully plan their recovery foods and fluids—particularly if they are doing double sessions and/or competing in tournament situations.

When soccer is intense, be sure to plan your recovery diet, just as you plan your pre-game meal. You need carbs and water to rapidly refuel your muscles and rehydrate your body. Ideally, you should also consume a little protein, to reduce muscle soreness and help repair damaged muscles. If your next game is two hours away, you should immediately consume some chocolate milk, instant breakfast, yogurt, juice, sports drink, or even a soft drink if all else fails.

Your muscles are 60% more efficient in rebuilding their glycogen stores if you can refuel 30 to 60 minutes after activity. However, many players are stuck without any refreshments conveniently nearby. Plan ahead to have your post-game recovery food handy.

All too often, exhausted soccer players say they are "too tired to eat." Or, they have traveled to a game and are eager to get home. Perhaps they have no food in the car and don't want to stop to eat. Or, they might be weight-conscious and hesitant to refuel. After a hard workout that "kills" their appetite, they may have little desire to eat, so they ignore all advice to rapidly refuel. Unfortunately, they miss the opportunity to speed muscle recovery and many of them end up devouring cookies or other junk food in a few hours when hunger strikes.

Recovery Options

What should you eat to optimize recovery after an intense session? Any fuel is better than no fuel, but the best post-exercise snacks include a foundation of carbs to replace the depleted glycogen stores, and a small amount protein to repair the muscle damage.

A 125-pound (57 kg) exhausted player should graze on about 250 to 350 calories of carbs within the first half hour, and then again every two hours for the next four to six hours. More precisely, the target is ~0.5 to 0.7 grams of carbohydrate per pound of body weight (~1.0 to 1.5 g carb/kg) or ~750 to 1,400 calories (~200 to 350 g) of recovery carbs. That may seem like a lot of bagels, pretzels, bananas and juice, but your appetite will guide the way.

Assuming you are not "dieting" nor are "too busy" to eat, you'll tend to naturally follow a pattern with repeated doses of simple snacks. Some popular carb + protein recovery choices include:

Fruit yogurt + Grape-Nuts
Chocolate milk
Cereal with milk
Turkey on a bulky roll
Pita and hummus
Toasted (low-fat) cheese and tomato sandwich
Chicken dinner with rice and vegetables
Spaghetti with meatballs
Bean burritos

If you are refueling after an away-game or during a tournament, carry with you such foods as:

Trail mix (nuts and raisins)
Bagel with peanut butter and jelly
Go-gurt (liquid yogurt)
Apple and cheese sticks
Energy bar with 3 to 4 times as many carbs as protein

If the weather is cold, pack a thermos filled with warm minestrone or chicken noodle soup. In hot weather, think cold beverages and chilled fruit with cottage cheese and crackers.

KRISTINE LILLY'S RECOVERY FOODS

Here's what Boston Breakers player Kristine Lilly commonly uses to refuel after a hard game. She tosses the food into her soccer bag, so it is ready and waiting to be devoured!

Chocolate Gatorade Shake
Chocolate Chip Fiber-One Bar
Water
Sandwich of some sort (like her favorite PB&J, made with soft bread, raspberry jelly and peanut butter)

Some soccer players like commercial recovery drinks, like Accelerade or Endurox. Just remember: these engineered foods lack all the health-protective nutrients that you get in "real food," so be sure to balance them into an overall healthful diet. Or, choose meal replacers like Carnation Instant Breakfast, Boost, Slim Fast or Ensure, because they offer more nutritional value.

If you have over-extended yourself and feel nauseous after a tough game, try to take in some chicken soup, or drink a little ginger ale while nibbling on a few saltines or pretzels. The sooner you can get fluids, carbs and sodium into your system, the better you will start to feel.

How much should you drink? If you are a recreational player and have consumed adequate pre-event liquids, you will unlikley be exercising to the extent you become dehydrated. But if you play intensely in the heat, you should replace fluid losses as soon as possible to help your body restore normal water balance.

As to what to drink after a workout:

- Water generally does the job of replacing sweat losses for both youth and competitive players; the accompanying recovery snacks can offer the needed carbs, protein and sodium.

- Sports drinks, while popular after exercise, are actually designed to be consumed during exercise that lasts for longer than 60 to 90 minutes. Sports drinks can be enjoyed post-exercise, but real foods tend to offer more nutritional value and electrolytes (sodium, potassium).

- Chocolate milk, fruit smoothies (made with blenderized fruit + yogurt), and Instant Breakfast drinks are excellent for exhausted players who need to rapidly refuel with a carb-protein combination.

Popular Recovery Foods

Your muscles are most receptive to replacing depleted glycogen stores immediately after exercise. By feeding them carbohydrates, preferably with a little bit of protein, you can optimize the recovery process. Don't get hung-up on the recommended 4 to 1 ratio of carbs to protein; just enjoy wholesome carb-based foods that will refuel depleted glycogen stores. Include a little protein to repair and build muscles, but do not emphasize the protein.

Depleted soccer players should consume at least 60 to 90 grams of carbs within the first half-hour or so.

Some sample choices include:

Fluids (8 oz; 240 ml):	Carb (g)	Protein (g)
Gatorade	14	--
Cranberry juice	43	--
Accelerade	14	3
Chocolate milk	26	8
Yogurt, flavored	40	10
Solids:		
Trail mix (raisins, granola, nuts)	40	10
PowerBar, chocolate	45	10
Cheerios w/ milk	50	12
Pasta, 2 cups + meat sauce	100	20

Do You Need Extra Salt to Replace What You Lose in Sweat?

As a recreational player who exercises for about an hour, you are unlikely to be losing gallons of sweat, nor significant amounts of sodium. Your standard diet undoubtedly offers more than enough sodium.

Even if you are in a tournament and sweating heavily for two or three hours, you are unlikely to become sodium depleted. You might lose about 1,800 to 5,600 milligrams of sodium, but the average 150-pound person's body contains about 97,000 milligrams of sodium. Hence, a small 2 to 6% loss is relatively insignificant.

However, if you are a salty sweater, and find yourself craving salt, you should indeed respond appropriately by eating salty foods such as salted pretzels, soups, crackers and/or salt sprinkled on baked potatoes or other foods. There is no harm in enjoying salty foods post-exercise. If you tend to avoid the saltshaker, as well as processed (high-sodium) foods, you might feel better with a bit more salt added to your diet.

Instead of replacing sodium after the game, choose some salty foods, like chicken noodle soup or a ham and cheese sandwich, *before* the soccer session. These will help your body retain fluid and reduce the risk of dehydration. If you repeatedly experience muscle cramps, experiment with boosting your sodium intake on a daily basis, especially if you are doing hard workouts and extended training in the summer heat.

"I sweat a ton and lose a lot of salt when I play. I usually crave salty food after games. The salt tastes good and helps me feel better."

Rachel Buehler, Defender, FC Gold Pride

Do You Need Extra Protein?

While eating a little protein along with recovery carbohydrates is a smart choice, you should not "protein load" by eating a protein-based recovery diet. That is, do not choose a protein bar or protein shake for your recovery food. Instead, have a carb shake (i.e., a fruit smoothie made with yogurt and fruit, such as those in the Recipe Section) that offers a foundation of carbs with a bit of protein. Remember: the need for carbs to refuel your muscles is greater than the need for protein to repair muscles. Eating too much protein can displace the carbs from your diet.

"I always try to refuel with some carbs and protein—like a banana and a protein bar—after a hard game or workout. This helps my muscles recover quicker."

Kelly Smith, Forward, Boston Breakers

Remember to Take Rest Days

Rest is an essential part of a soccer training program. If you feel compelled to train hard every day to try to improve your soccer skills, think again! Daily intense exercise hinders your muscles' ability to fully refuel. While one rest day allows time for muscles to refuel fairly well, some researchers encourage three days for optimal muscle recovery, particularly if you have depleted yourself (Ispirlidis).

Summary

If you are in a soccer camp, pre-season training, or at a tournament—all scenarios that require intense day-to-day play—remember to take the extra steps needed to eat and drink wisely. Refueling with the right foods is very important. You'll feel more energetic the rest of the day if you refuel properly. You may reduce post-exercise muscle soreness.

Also, your muscles will be better able to repair the damage or minor injuries that may have occurred during the soccer session, and your body will be better able to endure repeated days (and hopefully months and years) of games that will get progressively longer and more intense. Recreational or novice players can pave the way for more advanced play by getting a "sports nutrition education" and developing good habits.

Chapter 13
Tips for Tournaments and Traveling Soccer Players

Participating in a tournament that is far from home provides a fun opportunity to travel and compete. But all too often when traveling, you can get nutritionally sidetracked by the confusion and excitement of being on the road. You'll want to pre-plan how you are going to best fuel yourself. Some players and their families or teammates travel with a cooler packed with abundant tried-and-true meals and snacks. Others confront the nutritional challenges of finding familiar sports foods at local restaurants and stores. Whatever you do, remember that in a tournament situation, every meal is a pre-game meal. Even if you're not yet at this point in your soccer career, it's still good to gain an understanding, so you can develop good sports nutrition and lifestyle habits early on.

Eating for Tournaments or "The Big Game"

If you are about to embark on some serious back-to-back games, training, or even important try-outs, you want to be sure your muscles are fully fueled. This entails a type of "carbohydrate loading" similar to what endurance athletes, like marathoners or triathletes, practice before big events. Here are some tips on getting the job done. Eating a high-carbohydrate diet means more than just stuffing yourself with pasta; a good sports diet ensures adequate "muscle and mind" fuel. You should not change your tried-and-true diet for these events, but rather, just be more focused on executing sports nutrition principles.

Daily training diet
Eat a carbohydrate-rich sports diet *every* day as the foundation for *every* meal to develop a tried-and-true training diet that will support your soccer aspirations.
- Try to train at the same time you'll be competing.
- Before practices, eat your planned pre-competition meal.
- Learn how much pre-exercise food you can eat and then still play comfortably.
- Practice consuming the sports drink that will be available during the tournament as well as any mid-game foods (sports gels, fruit) you plan to eat.

The week before the tournament:
- Cut back on your training so that your muscles have the opportunity to become fully loaded with fuel.
- Keep your eating about the same leading up to the big day(s). The 600 to 1,000 calories you generally expend during training will be used to fuel your muscles.
- Be sure that you are *carbo*-loading, not *fat*-loading. That is, instead of having one roll with butter for 200 calories, have two plain rolls for 200 calories. Enjoy pasta with tomato sauce rather than oily or cheesy toppings.
- Continue to eat a small serving of low-fat proteins as the *accompaniment* to the meal (not the main focus).

"Rather than stuffing myself right before a game, I try to eat a lot 48 hours before and then 24 hours. On game day, I eat—but not tons— so I can then feel a little bit lighter on my feet."

Tina Ellertson, Defender, Saint Louis Athletica

The day before the tournament

- Instead of relying upon a huge pasta dinner the night before the tournament, you might want to enjoy a substantial carb-based meal at breakfast or lunch on game day. This earlier meal allows plenty of time for the food to move through your system. Or, depending on game times, eat your carb-fest at both times!
- Drink extra water, juices, and even carbohydrate-rich sports drinks, if desired.
- Expect to gain possibly about 2 to 4 pounds of *water weight*. For every ounce of carbohydrate stored in your body, you store about three ounces of water.

Game morning

- Eat a tried-and-true breakfast that will settle well.
- Drink plenty of fluids. Take your preferred beverage with you so you'll have it available at the game.
- If you are a coffee, tea or cocoa drinker, enjoy your standard morning beverage.

During the tournament

- Prevent dehydration by drinking on a schedule as much as possible.
- Maintain a normal blood sugar level by consuming about 200 to 300 calories of carbs during the game, in addition to having fueled up before and after, especially on multi-game days.

Note: These topics are discussed in detail in Chapters 8, 10 and 11.

Sample High Carbohydrate Menus #1

	Breakfast	Lunch	Pre-play Snack	Dinner
Menu #1	Wheaties Milk, 1% low-fat Bagel Honey Orange juice	Whole-grain bread, 2 slices Peanut butter Jelly Fruit yogurt Pretzels	Apple Graham crackers	Chicken breast Rice Broccoli Dinner roll Sherbet

Sample High Carbohydrate Menus #2

	Breakfast	Lunch	Pre-play Snack	Dinner
Menu #2	Oatmeal Milk Raisins Brown sugar Apple juice	Baguette Lean meat Lettuce, tomato Fruit yogurt Grape juice	Fig Newtons Low-fat milk	Spaghetti Tomato sauce with a little meat Italian bread Salad with lite dressing (Canned) peaches or fresh fruit

Eating on the Road

To help you better accommodate a healthful high-carbohydrate sports diet during your traveling routine, here are a few tips.

Breakfast:
- At a restaurant, order pancakes, French toast, whole-wheat toast, or English, bran, or corn muffins. Add jelly, jam, or maple syrup for extra carbohydrates, but hold the butter or request that it be served on the side so that you can better control the amount of fat in your meal. Add a little protein to the muffin or toast meal, such as eggs (or egg whites) or a glass of low-fat or skim milk.
- Order a *large* orange juice or tomato juice. This can help compensate for a potential lack of fruits or veggies in the other meals.
- Try to stay in a hotel that offers a free breakfast. If it doesn't, pre-arrange a group deal. If the game is very early, request a packed-to-go breakfast (bagel, banana, yogurt) or ask if the hotel can accommodate a group request for an earlier meal.

Easier yet, for a hotel stay, you might want to save time and money by packing your own cereal, raisins, and spoon. Either bring powdered milk or buy a half-pint of low-fat milk at a local convenience store. A water glass or milk carton can double as a cereal bowl. Or, you can check out supermarkets in the area upon arriving, and stock up. Consider volunteers buying for the entire team.

Lunch:

- Find a deli or restaurant that offers wholesome breads. Request a sandwich that emphasizes the bread, rather than the filling (preferably lean beef, turkey, ham, or chicken). Go easy on the mayonnaise, and instead, add moistness with mustard or ketchup, sliced tomatoes, and lettuce. Add more carbohydrates with juice, fruit, fig bars (brought from a corner store), or yogurt for dessert.
- At fast-food restaurants, the burgers, fried fish, special sandwiches, and French fries have a very high fat content. You'll get more carbohydrates by sticking to the spaghetti, baked potatoes, bean chili, or thick-crust pizza selections.
- Request thick-crust pizza (with veggie toppings) rather than thin-crust pizza with pepperoni or sausage. If thin crust, then order without the meats, and add a side salad if desired.
- At a salad bar, generously pile on the chickpeas, three-bean salad, beets, and fat-free croutons. Take plenty of bread. But don't fat-load on large amounts of butter, salad dressings, and mayonnaise-smothered pasta and potato salads.
- Baked potatoes are a super choice if you request them plain rather than drenched with butter, lots of sour cream, and cheese toppings. For moistness, try mashing the potato with milk rather than butter, or eat them with ketchup. A small amount of sour cream and salt to taste is not a bad alternative.
- Hearty soups (such as split pea, minestrone, lentil, vegetable, or noodle) accompanied by crackers, bread, a plain bagel, or an English muffin provide a satisfying, carbohydrate-rich, low-fat meal.
- Both juices and soft drinks are rich in carbohydrates. Juices, however, are nutritionally preferable for vitamin C, potassium, and wholesome goodness. It's better to teach players to limit soda.
- Save the typical fast food, candy and treats for after the games.

"When I'm travelling and on the run, I like to eat raw almonds. They are a really nutritious snack and provide good protein."

Rachel Buehler, Defender, FC Gold Pride

Dinner:

- If possible, check out the restaurant beforehand to make sure that it offers wholesome carbohydrates (pasta, baked potatoes, rice, steamed vegetables, salad bar, homemade breads, fruit, juice), broiled foods, and low-fat options.

Inquire how dishes are made. Request they be prepared with minimal fat (so also avoid heavy sauces). Let management know the time you'll arrive and number in your party to avoid long waits. Those waits can undermine your team's nutrition and general scheduling plan.

- Eat the breads and rolls either plain or with jelly. Replace the butter calories with high-carbohydrate choices: another slice of bread, a second potato, soup and crackers, juice, sherbet, or frozen yogurt.
- When ordering salads, always request the dressing be served on the side. Otherwise, you may get as many as 400 calories of oil or mayonnaise—fatty foods that fill your stomach but leave your muscles unfueled.

Snacks and munchies:
- Pack your own snacks. Some suggestions include: whole-grain bagels, muffins, rolls, crackers, pretzels, fig bars, energy bars, granola bars, oatmeal raisin cookies, graham crackers, oranges, raisins, dried or fresh fruit, and juice boxes.
- Buy wholesome snacks at a supermarket or convenience store: small packets of trail mix, bananas, dried fruit, yogurt, V-8 juice or fruit juice, bagel, hot pretzel, slice of thick-crust pizza, small sandwich, or cup of soup.

Tips for Parents, Managers and Coaches when Traveling with the Team

- Remind each player to bring her personal supply of emergency food and fluids. For insurance, request each player bring an extra filled large water bottle.
- If flying, have each player pack one or two empty water bottles to be refilled after going through airport security.
- If the team will be eating as a group, order a buffet-style meal, so each player can choose the foods she wants, and to be able to get the desired quantity.
- Find restaurants immediately after arriving to your destination. Ask if they can prepare to feed a large group (so you don't have to wait forever for service, give them a heads up) and if they can accommodate your group's sports food needs.
- Request pitchers of water be put on each table.
- Locate the local supermarket. Find a volunteer to buy snacks for the group. Ask for volunteers to organize team meals or snacks at game sites, if necessary.
- Provide fresh fruit, yogurt, granola bars, and juice boxes for snacks to be available in hotel rooms.
- Remind players to pack their plastic zip lock bag of non-perishable snacks in their soccer bags, so it is with them at all times. And then, not to forget to eat those snacks!

Pack it to Go, and Carry it With You!

Packing your tried-and-true sports meals and snacks in a cooler is an ideal way to carry your food with you everywhere. (You can restock on the road by refreezing your ice packs in hotels.) But players often find themselves stuck without timely access to those coolers. After all, parents, and their cars, aren't always with their players, so many of them miss a window of opportunity to eat because of field location, game schedule, etc. Make use of the many convenient thermal options: various sized silver bags sold in supermarkets; neoprene or other type lunch bags, etc. Choose a thermal bag that can be folded small enough to fit in your soccer bag or backpack. Also, freeze bottles of water or sports drink and put them in with your snack. The drink will melt enough to be drinkable, but stay cold enough to keep food chilled. (Put the bottle in a plastic bag, to catch the "sweat" so the rest of your food will stay dry.)

"It's important to know your routine, and what suits you best for game day."

Kelly Smith, Forward, Boston Breakers

SAFE PLASTICS

There's a lot of plastic when packing to go. In Gloria's early years of organizing for soccer, there wasn't the same wealth of information on how to do it as safely as possible. Now, we know more. When you need to use plastic, these are the safer choices to use with food: 1, 2, 4 and 5. Learn to recognize, and then avoid, polycarbonate (number 7) for food usage. Polycarbonate plastics are hard and clear.

If you must use plastic wrap, make sure it is a brand free of both BPA and PVC. Ziploc, Glad and Saran Wrap are promoted as being free of BPA and PVC.

Summary

Traveling is fun but filled with food temptations. Do your best to stick to tried-and-true foods that you know will settle well and not upset your digestive system. Save the less sports-oriented food until *after* the games are over.

If you have any doubts about the availability of familiar foods, plan ahead and bring some "safe" foods with you—including the gels, energy bars, and sports snacks you will want to consume during the game itself, as well as pre-game and recovery snacks. That way, if you are presented with a meal that is all wrong for you (such as tournament donuts, burgers, hot dogs, fried chicken and French fries), you can at least supplement the high fat foods with carbs (e.g. fig cookies, dried pineapple, and baked chips). Think ahead, plan ahead, and be responsible. Make good nutrition your advantage for a successful tournament!

SECTION IV
WEIGHT AND SOCCER

Chapter 14
Calorie Needs of Soccer Players

Most soccer players are on the "see food diet." They see food and they eat it. They eat when they are hungry, stop when they are content and naturally regulate a proper calorie intake. This happens day in, day out, regardless of whether they are a 100-pound (45 kg) youth player who may need 2,000 calories or a 160 pound (75 kg) professional player who burns 4,000 calories a day (the equivalent of about two large cheese pizzas per day, or half a large pizza every 4 hours).

On the other hand, some weight-conscious soccer players see food and try to *not* eat it because they want to lose undesired body fat or or prevent undesired weight gain. They deem food as "fattening." They often undereat by day, but then commonly end up overeating at dinner. Or, they are concerned about gaining undesired body fat during the off-season, a time of low activity and often high food intake.

As an athlete, you want to fuel your body evenly throughout the day. If you need to lose weight, you can do that at night, when you are sleeping! (See Chapter 16.) You want to eat *enough* at breakfast and lunch to support your basic needs, an active lifestyle, and your training program. Eating (wholesome) calories evenly throughout the day invests in high energy, added stamina, strength, and successful playing, to say nothing of better health.

If you struggle with energy lags late morning or mid-afternoon, you might want to assess how many calories you are eating at breakfast and lunch, and then compare that to how many calories your body requires. Just as knowing how much money you can spend when you go shopping is helpful, knowing your calorie budget can also be helpful—*if* you are disconnected from your body's ability to naturally regulate an appropriate food intake. Knowing your calorie budget can help you determine how much your body requires to:
• maintain even energy throughout the day, from morning through evening.
• fuel-up and refuel from workouts.
• exercise longer and stronger.
• lose desired weight and maintain energy for soccer.
• feel good about your eating—no guilt for enjoying those pancakes for breakfast.

Knowledge of calorie needs can be particularly helpful to soccer players who feel tired all the time. It can help you understand *why* you are tired. For example, if your body requires 2,400 calories a day, and you skip breakfast and then eat only 200 calories of a granola bar for lunch, you can clearly see why you lack energy for your afternoon soccer practice—or worse yet, for a game during which you might burn off 500 to 1,500 calories (depending on your position and body size).

If you are weight-conscious, calorie information allows you to determine how much food you can eat for fuel, yet still lose body fat. Once you get in touch with how you feel when you eat appropriately, you'll be better able to regulate your food intake naturally—without counting calories. Ultimately, paying attention to hunger, fullness, energy and performance is more natural—and more important —than counting calories.

CALORIES AND MORE CALORIES

Youth soccer players are calorie-burning machines. Consider that an average youth player runs anywhere from 2 to 4 miles per game, while older players and pros can cover up to 10K (6.2 miles). If you compute for a typical two-day tournament, that's an amazing 10 to 15 miles per day for the youth player. Running alone burns 100 calories per mile (the equivalent of a medium banana). Toss in the other demands of the sport, the caloric requirements of just growing and existing, and you can appreciate that playing this game requires enormous energy expenditure.

In one British study of top 14-year-old swimmers, soccer players, and track athletes, all three groups failed to meet the recommendations for caloric intake (at least 3,000 calories per day for active young athletes). Soccer players were also deficient in vitamin D, zinc, calcium, magnesium, and iron. Nutritional knowledge was also low, as a questionnaire revealed. From a possible score of 56 points, soccer players averaged 15.5.

We encourage you to think of yourself as an endurance athlete—like a cyclist or marathoner —with "a banana in one hand and a sandwich in the other." Basically, you should feel like you are eating "all the time." This is because most youth players fail to eat enough. They are distracted, nervous or excited, and not focusing on food. Or, they eat a normal amount—for a sedentary person.

"My nutrition advice to young players is to not listen to what the average person says about dieting, because the average person does not burn the same amount of calories as a soccer player. Rather, listen to your body. You know how you feel when your blood sugar is low. If you feel that way during practice or a game, you need more calories. However, if you feel a bit full before a game or practice, you are probably eating too much."

Cat Whitehill, Defender, Washington Freedom

Calculating Your Calorie Needs

Here's an easy formula to help you estimate your calorie needs. For more personalized advice, we highly recommend you or your team consult with a registered dietitian (RD) who specializes in sports nutrition. To find a local nutrition professional, use the American Dietetic Association's referral network at **www.eatright.org** or **www.SCANdpg.org**.

1. To estimate your resting metabolic rate (RMR), that is, the amount of calories you need to simply breathe, pump blood, and be alive:

   Multiply your weight (or a good weight for your body) by 10 calories per pound (or 22 calories per kilogram).

   _____weight (lbs) x 10 calories/lb = _____ calories for your RMR (resting metabolic rate)

Example: If you weigh 120 pounds, you need approximately 1,200 calories (120 x 10) to simply do nothing all day except exist. (If you are significantly overweight, use an adjusted weight: the weight that is halfway between your desired weight and your current weight.)

2. Add more calories for daily activity—apart from your training and other purposeful exercise.

- 50% x RMR if you are moderately active throughout the day (apart from soccer)
- ~30-40% if you are sedentary
- ~60-70% if you are very active

   50% x _____RMR = _____ calories for daily activity

Example: A moderately active 120-pound soccer player requires about 1,200 calories for the resting metabolic rate and another 600 more calories for activities of daily living. This totals 1,800 calories per day—without soccer.

3. Add more calories for your purposeful exercise. The number of calories you need depends on your position (obviously, goalkeepers demand fewer calories than field players), your body weight, and your intensity of exercise. A 120-pound player who trains hard might need 500 or more calories during an hour of exertion; a 160-pound player might burn 700 or more calories per hour. During a highly competitive game, a player may run 5 to 7 miles and burn 1,100 calories (women) to 1,500 calories (men). See **www.caloriesperhour.com** for more specific calorie information.

____exercise calories + _____daily activity + _____RMR = _____total calories

Example: A 120-pound soccer player who trains only moderately hard at a $1^{1}/_{2}$ hour-practice (during which she is standing one third of the time) may burn about 400 calories during the session. This brings her to about 2,200 calories per day to maintain her weight (400 soccer + 600 moderate daily activity + 1,200 RMR = 2,200).

Note: After a hard workout, soccer athletes tend to rest, recover and burn fewer calories than usual during the rest of their day. Observe if this happens with you. That is, notice if you are more sedentary (reading, TV, computer) after having done a tiring practice session. While you need that rest and relaxation to regroup, you'll also need to adjust your calorie requirements accordingly.

Also, pay attention to your activity levels during the off-season. Some players continue to eat the same size portions (e.g. the large ice cream cone) even though they are far less active.

4. To lose weight, target 80 to 90% of total calorie needs.

80% x _____total calories = _____ calories to reduce weight

Example: .80 x 2,200 calories = 1,760 calories, or more simply 1,800 calories/day

(Refer to Chapter 16 for more guidance on weight loss.)

5. Now, take your calorie budget and divide it into three or four parts of the day. For the 120-pound female, this comes to:

	Calories			Calories
Breakfast/snack	800	OR	Breakfast	600
Lunch/snack	800		Lunch	600
Dinner/snack	800		Lunch #2	600
			Dinner	600

The next step is to read food labels and get calorie information from websites such as www.fitday.com or www.calorieking.com to become familiar with the calorie content of the foods you commonly eat. Now, fuel your body according to the rules for a well-balanced diet.

(**Take Note:** We are NOT recommending diets; we are encouraging players to eat —but eat just a little less if they have excess body fat. Ideally, soccer has helped the players acquire a positive body image. Read on for more on this topic).

"As athletes, we're training two and a half to three hours a day. We need to put calories in, so for me it's not about limiting what I can eat, it's about eating enough."

Hope Solo, 2009 Coast Guard Goalkeeper of the Year, Saint Louis Athletica

Hungry All the Time?

We commonly hear soccer players complain, "Once the soccer season starts, I'm hungry all the time." They often feel confused by hunger and sometimes even feel guilty they are always eager to eat.

Hunger is normal; it is simply your body's way of talking to you, requesting fuel. After all, the more you exercise, the hungrier you will get and the more fuel you'll need. Plan to fuel up or refuel at least every four hours. You should not spend your day feeling hungry—even if you are on a reducing diet. If your 8:00 A.M. breakfast finds you hungry by 10:00, your breakfast simply contained too few calories. You need a supplemental midmorning snack or a bigger breakfast that supplies about 25% to 35% of your day's calories.

Come noontime, instead of thinking something is wrong with you because you are hungry again, enjoy lunch as the second-most-important meal of the day. Morning exercisers, in particular, need a hearty lunch to refuel their muscles; afternoon exercisers need a respectable lunch and afternoon snack/second lunch to fuel for their afternoon training.

Whereas some soccer players like to satisfy their appetites with big meals, others prefer to divide their calories into mini-meals eaten every two hours. Eat however suits your training schedule and lifestyle. But whatever you do, eat when you are physically hungry. Hunger is simply your body's request for fuel. (Chapter 17 offers strategies for managing over-eating, that is, mis-using food as a "drug" to calm and reward yourself.)

"I LOVE TO EAT, and being an athlete, I am hungry ALL THE TIME! I have even named my stomach 'the beast'! When I get hungry, I tell my teammates, 'It's time to feed the beast'!"

Kendall Fletcher, Midfielder, Saint Louis Athletica

Summary

Just as you know how much money you can spend when you shop, some players find it helpful to know how many calories they can enjoy spending when they eat. Weight-conscious players, in particular, tend to undereat during the day and overeat at night. By targeting an appropriate (and often larger than normal) breakfast and lunch, soccer players can fuel themselves evenly throughout the day, learn to listen to hunger cues, and respond by eating appropriately-sized meals and snacks. Calorie-counting should be a tool to get in touch with how much is okay to eat (as opposed to how little they can survive on).

Chapter 15
Bulking Up Healthfully

If you are thin, and worried about becoming even leaner as the season goes on, especially if you are still growing, you need to eat responsibly to keep up with your calorie needs.

The more you exercise, the more you'll want to eat—assuming you make the time and preparations to do so. A hard training session or game may temporarily "kill" your appetite, but within a few hours, after you have cooled down, you will become plenty hungry. In the meantime, remember that soccer is a game with a role for every body: big and small. Thinner players often make up in skill for what they may lack in size. Here are a few tips to help you boost calories and prevent undesired weight loss.

"When you are smaller than the other players, you have to work more and play with a lot of patience and intensity. I use my smarts and compensate with my brain, cleverness, and intelligence."

Sonia Bompastor, Defender/Midfielder, Washington Freedom

Six Tips for Boosting Calories

1. Eat consistently.
Have at least three hearty meals plus two or three additional snacks/meals daily. If you will miss opportunities to eat, carry snacks or a travel mug with a liquid lunch, like a smoothie or meal replacement drink.

If you are spending a significant amount of time traveling to and from soccer games, you may need to be creative and turn your car or soccer bag into a pantry. Keep it stocked with non-perishable snacks like granola bars, raisins, dried fruits, nuts, trail mix, juice boxes, fig bars and other pre-packaged snacks. This way, you'll have more time to munch on calories that might otherwise get squeezed out of your busy day.

If you or your parents tend to come back from practices or games "too tired to cook," plan ahead and have a meal all prepared and waiting to be heated.
If you arrive home "too tired to eat," prepare a quart of Carnation Instant Breakfast or similar liquid meal before your workout, so it will be in the refrigerator. For an exhausted athlete, swigging a liquid meal can be easier than eating solid food. Along with that liquid meal, nibble on bite-sized calorie-dense finger foods, like a bowl of trail mix or (low-fat) cheese and crackers. This can be an easier source of calories than knife-and-fork meals that seem like a lot of effort, especially if you are the one who needs to prepare them.

2. Eat larger portions.

Some players think they need to buy expensive weight-gain powders to bulk up. Not the case; standard foods work fine. The only reason commercial powders "work" is because they provide additional calories. For example, one soccer player religiously drank the recommended three glasses a day of a 300-calorie weight-gain shake; he consumed an extra 900 calories. Although he credited the shake for helping boost his weight, he could have less expensively consumed those calories via supermarket foods.

Nancy suggested that he simply eat larger portions of his standard fare. Doing so, he met his goal of 1,000 extra calories per day and continued to see the desired results—less expensively.

3. Select higher calorie foods, but not higher fat foods.

Excess calories of dietary fat easily convert into body fat. This fattens you up rather than bulks up your muscles. And it is unhealthy if you chow on ice cream, cookies and chips. But you can boost calories by adding *healthful* fats to your diet, such as avocadoes, nuts, olive and canola oil.

A wise bet for extra calories is to choose carbohydrate-dense foods that have more calories than an equally desirable counterpart (e.g. cranberry juice has more carbs and calories than orange juice). (See sidebar below). By reading food labels, you'll be able to make the best choices.

How to Boost Your Calories

Choose more:	Calories	Amount	Instead of:	Calories	Amount
Cranberry juice	170	8 oz (240 ml)	Orange juice	110	8 ounces
Grape juice	160	8 oz (240 ml)	Grapefruit juice	100	8 ounces
Banana	170	1 large	Apple	130	1 large
Granola	780	1.5 cups (150 g)	Bran flakes	200	1.5 cups (60 g)
Grape-Nuts	660	1.5 cups (175 g)	Cheerios	160	1.5 cups (45 g)
Corn	140	1 cup (165 g)	Green beans	40	1 cup (120 g)
Carrots	45	1 cup (150 g)	Zucchini	30	1 cup (180 g)
Split pea soup	130	1 cup (240 ml)	Vegetable soup	80	1 cup (240 g)
Baked beans	260	1 cup (260 g)	Rice	190	1 cup (160 g)

4. Drink lots of juice and low-fat milk.

Beverages are a simple way to increase your calorie intake. Replace part or all of the water you drink with calorie-containing fluids. (You don't need to drink water to get adequate water; e.g. juice is 99% water.) Extra juices are not only a great source of calories and fluids, but also of carbohydrates to keep your muscles well fueled. Fruit smoothies fortified with powdered milk are another option.

If you are a growing teenage soccer player, plan to drink at least four 8-ounce glasses of milk a day (or their equivalent from other high-calcium sources) to get the calcium you need for your growing bones. By simply enjoying 16 ounces of chocolate milk for a recovery food, which many athletes drink after playing, you'll be halfway to your calcium- and additional-calorie goals for the day.

5. Do strength training (push-ups, weightlifting) to stimulate muscular development.

As discussed in Chapter 6, you don't need to eat slabs of meat or protein-rich foods to build muscles. You want to eat protein-rich foods (to build muscles) as an accompaniment to a foundation of carbohydrates (to fuel muscles).

Strength training is essential if you want to bulk up (instead of fatten up). Resistance exercise is the key to muscular development. Most serious players include a strength program in their training, but even if you are a young beginner, a few simple exercises can strengthen your muscles, enhance your soccer program, and help prevent injury. Consult a soccer-specific trainer for assistance in creating a program.

6. Be patient.

If you are a thin young player, your physique will undoubtedly fill out as you get older. Know that you can be a strong and powerful soccer athlete by being well fueled and well trained. Be aware that your skinny legs may hurt your self-esteem more than your athletic ability. The beauty of the game is that you can be successful at it no matter your size or shape, and also, over time, you will develop a toned and strong physique simply by playing the game—and, of course, by following a good sports diet.

Summary

The key to gaining weight is to consistently consume more calories that you currently enjoy. Simple ways to do this include choosing certain calorie-dense foods, eating larger portions at meals (particularly breakfast and lunch, because dinners tend to be large enough), and replacing water with juices and low-fat milk. Strength training is an important part of a weight gain and sports program, so you add more muscle than fat.

Chapter 16
Getting Lighter and Leaner

If you are a young female player or her family or coach reading this, we want to
say right up front that for all the obvious reasons, we do not endorse any type of
dieting for these players. The goal of eating well, which we outline in this book,
is to achieve a healthy, natural weight. However, for those older players who want
to sensibly achieve a weight goal, read on.

Among soccer athletes, a lean physique is often desirable for speed and agility. However, in addition to skill, soccer is also a game of strength and power, for which size can be an asset. Still, some players want to lose a little undesired body fat, hoping lightness will enhance their performance. They commonly assume excess body fat will simply melt away once the soccer season starts, but in-season can be a tough time to lose undesired weight; you need to eat well to have the energy to play hard.

"If you want to lose a few pounds, NEVER try to lose it during the hardest part of your season. Pre-season or off-season are the best times to do this. I have a personal experience of trying to lose too much weight during a crucial part of my Olympic team build-up, and I tore my ACL because of pushing my body too hard."

Cat Whitehill, Defender, Washington Freedom

How to Lose Weight and Have Energy to Exercise

Nancy spends hours helping all types of athletes who are fighting the battle of the bulge. Most think they should follow a strict diet with rigid rules and regulations. Wrong. Diets don't work. If diets did work, every athlete who has ever dieted would be as thin as desired.

The key to losing weight is to:
- stop thinking about *going* on a *diet.*
- start learning *how* to eat *healthfully.*
- trust that *appropriate eating + regular exercise* will lead to an *appropriate weight.*

How Much is Okay to Eat?

As outlined in Chapter 14, most soccer players can lose weight on 1,800 to 2,200 calories (or even more). This is far from a starvation diet! Note that your body requires a significant amount of energy simply to exist: pump blood, breathe, produce urine, grow hair, and maintain your other bodily functions. Exercise boosts your calorie needs, but often not as much as you may expect, particularly if you are a goalkeeper or reserve player.

To lose weight, you want to cut back on your food intake by just a little bit less (for example, drink less soda, use less butter) while you add on exercise. Don't get over-zealous and cut your food intake in half, with hopes of losing weight quickly. That's a big mistake. Soccer players who try to lose weight quickly tend to get too hungry, lag on energy, "blow their diets," and end up regaining weight quickly. Overtraining to burn extra calories is also a risk.

Food records (a diary) can be extremely useful to help you understand why you have gained weight in the first place and what you need to do to lose it. For example, by recording *everything* you eat, you might notice that you:
- munch when watching TV and don't even notice the portion.
- eat too little at breakfast and lunch, only to overindulge at night.
- diet Monday through Thursday, then splurge when tailgating after weekend games.
- If you are willing to keep accurate food records, you will probably be more successful with your weight reduction program. That's because people who keep food records tend to eat about 20% fewer calories, and that is a sustainable reducing diet.

If you are still growing, however, you should safely be able to follow your appetite, and with activity and good eating habits, you should not be concerned with dieting.

Five Keys to Successful Weight Reduction

You can lose weight with the following five keys to successful weight reduction.

Key #1. Eat just a little bit less at the end of the day. Don't get too hungry or you'll blow your diet.
The less you eat during the day, the more likely you are to blow your diet. Even if you can successfully restrict your intake, the less you eat, the more your body

adjusts to having fewer calories. You will start to conserve energy—similar to what a bear does in winter when food is scarce. That is, your metabolic rate will drop and you'll feel lethargic, cold, moody, and lack energy to exercise hard. Soccer will feel like work, not play.

As mentioned above, many active female soccer players can be successful with 1,800- to 2,200-calorie reducing diets. This is far more than their self-imposed 800- to 1,200-calorie starvation diets that often end in food binges. By simply knocking out fried foods (fried chicken, chips, French fries), sugary drinks, and fatty foods (butter, mayonnaise, excess salad dressing), you can create a small but effective calorie deficit that results in losing $1/_2$ to 1 pound per week for women, and 1 to 2 pounds per week for men. This rate of weight loss is realistic, allows you to eat enough carbs to fuel your muscles, and also have enough energy to enjoy your soccer.

How can you tell when you've eaten the right amount—not too much, nor too little? At the end of dinner, you want to feel "not quite full"; you could eat more, but you could also stop eating and get on with your evening. This is much different than feeling obsessed with hunger. By slightly undereating in the evening, you will then wake up in the morning ready for breakfast—and a tiny bit lighter after having lost weight when you were sleeping.

Key #2. Be sure that you fuel adequately during the day, so that you'll be able to eat less (diet) at night. For an appropriate reducing program, Nancy recommends you eat even-sized meals about every four hours throughout the day. Your goal is to eat on a schedule that prevents hunger. An appropriate eating pattern for a 1,800 to 2,200-calorie *reduction* diet might look like this:

	Time	Calories
Breakfast:	8 A.M.	500 to 600
Lunch:	Noon	500 to 600
Lunch #2/Snack:	4 P.M.	400
Soccer:	6 P.M.	
Dinner:	8 P.M.	400 to 600

This suggested meal plan may encourage you to consume more than you might be currently eating at breakfast, lunch, and afternoon snack/second lunch, but less at dinner (and little or nothing after dinner). You should eat enough to feel content after the first three meals, and not quite full after dinner.

Your training program may require a creative eating schedule if you play during meal times. If you have soccer practice at 6 P.M.—potentially at the height of your hunger—you will enjoy your session more if you eat part of your dinner before you practice. You could trade in your 100-calorie dinner potato for a 100-calorie banana at 5:00 P.M. Similarly, if you exercise at 8:00 A.M., you will enjoy greater energy if you eat part of your breakfast beforehand, such as a slice of toast and a glass of juice, and then eat a yogurt with granola afterwards to recover from the workout and satisfy your hunger.

(As mentioned in Chapter 10, experiment with pre-exercise food to determine the right amount to boost your energy without making you feel heavy and sluggish.) Players believe that exercising "on empty"—for example, running first thing in the morning before breakfast—helps them to burn more fat. While this may be true, keep in mind that *burning* fat does not equate to *losing* body fat. To lose body fat, you need to create a calorie deficit for the entire day (not just during workouts). If you exercise on empty, you'll lack the fuel you need to play longer and stronger. (Hence, you'll burn fewer calories since you'll be less active than if you had eaten adequately before you started to play, so you could play with full energy.) You may also experience extreme hunger later in the day and end up raiding the cookie jar.

Key #3. Eat an appropriate amount of fat. If you are currently eating a high-fat diet filled with butter, mayonnaise, salad dressing, French fries, and pepperoni, you should cut back on these and other fatty foods. Excess dietary fat easily turns into excess body fat, if not clogged arteries.

On the other hand, if you are trying to cut *all* the fat out of your diet—thinking that if you eat fat, you'll instantly gain body fat—think again and see Chapter 7. Fat can be helpful for dieters because it takes longer to digest and provides a nice feeling of satisfaction that can prevent you from scrounging around the kitchen, looking for something junky to eat. Soccer players who try to eat a very low fat diet commonly live with a nagging hunger, to say nothing of feelings of denial and deprivation.

One study reported that dieters who were instructed to eat 1,200 calories of a high-fat diet actually lost more body fat than the group who were instructed to eat 1,200 calories of a very low-fat diet. Why? Because the high-fat dieters were better able to comply with their regimen. You, too, may enjoy better success with weight loss if you give yourself a reasonable calorie and fat budget to spend on the foods that you truly enjoy eating. (Refer to Chapter 7 for more information on what a 25% fat diet looks like.) There is a diet portion of any food, including pizza and peanut butter! (And there is particularly room for healthy fats from such sources as avocados, salmon and nuts).

Key #4. Try to lose weight in the off-season, when life is calm. Stressful schedules (such as when you are juggling school/work and soccer) are often poor times to try to reduce body fat. When life is stressful, you may need to let go of your goal to lose fat and instead focus on not *gaining* weight. If you are both stressed and hungry, you can too easily succumb to overeating (even though obviously no amount of food will solve any life problem).

Why are You Eating?

Food has many roles. It satisfies hunger, fuels muscles, is a pleasurable part of social gatherings and celebrations, rewards us at the end of a stressful day, and has a calming effect. If you tend to eat for reasons other than hunger, think HALT and ask yourself, why am I eating? Am I—:

> Hungry?
>
> Angry or Anxious?
>
> Lonely?
>
> Tired?

If you are eating for reasons other than hunger, remember that no amount of food will solve any problem. Try not to start eating if you think you'll have problems stopping.

The off-season is the best time to lose weight, but is often the time when soccer players gain weight because they are less active and have more time to have fun with food and friends. If this has been your pattern, think twice before you eat. Ask yourself, "Does my body need this fuel?" Eat when you are hungry, but not when you are bored. The same holds true if you are injured. Many injured soccer players get depressed and try to cheer themselves up with chocolate and chips. Doesn't work. In fact, they end up more depressed because they now have gained undesired body fat. Not gaining weight is far easier than trying to lose it.

Key #5. Have realistic weight goals. Weight is more than a matter of willpower; genetics play a large role. If you are working out regularly, fueling appropriately during the day, eating lighter at night, and waking up hankering for breakfast— but still have not lost weight, perhaps you have an unrealistic weight goal. Maybe you have no excess fat to lose and are already lean for your genetic blueprint. You can remodel your body to a certain extent, but you cannot totally redesign it. Plain and simple, soccer players, like all people, come in varying sizes and shapes. No one body type is right or wrong. From the Atlanta Beat's first-ever draft (5 of those 7 players are 5'9" or over) to a slight Heather O'Reilly of Sky Blue FC—elite soccer players come in all sizes and shapes.

In order to determine an appropriate weight for your body, we recommend you stop looking at the scale and start looking at your family tree. Imagine yourself at a family reunion.

- How do you compare to other members of your family?
- Are you currently leaner than they are? Heavier? The same?
- If you are leaner, are you struggling to maintain that low weight?

If you are significantly leaner, you may already be underfat for your body.

The Slow Metabolism Woes

Some soccer players perceive themselves as being energy-efficient and having to eat "less than they deserve." They express these complaints:

- *I eat less than my friends but I still don't lose weight. There must be something wrong with my metabolism.*
- *I maintain weight on only 1,000 calories per day. I want to lose a few pounds, but I can't imagine eating any less.*
- *I train every day and eat only one meal a day. I can't understand why I don't lose weight.*

Does Nature slow an athlete's metabolism to protect her from getting too thin? Or, does the athlete become very inactive when she is not exercising? That is, after a hard soccer game, does the player take a nap, watch TV, or relax more than usual? Hence, the trick to reversing "energy efficiency" may simply be to remain active in a low-key fashion, by walking around or gently moving more throughout the entire day, not just when training.

Nancy counsels many athletes who struggle to lose the final few pounds. Some of them are simply trying to get to a weight that is abnormal for their genetics. For example, some female soccer players lament what they call their "fat thighs." They fail to understand that fat in the thigh area is sex-specific. It is a storehouse of fuel for potential pregnancy and breast-feeding and is *supposed* to be there. Just as women have breast tissue, women also have thigh tissue. Women have fatter thighs than men because women are *women*.

Target Weights

Although only nature knows the best weight for your body, the following guidelines offer a very general method to estimate a healthy weight range. Add or subtract 10%, according to your body frame and musculature. (Note: These guidelines do not work for very muscular soccer players.)

Women: 100 pounds (45 kg) for the first 5 feet (1.52 m) of height;
5 pounds (2.3 kg) per inch (2.5 cm) thereafter

Example: A woman who is 5'6" could appropriately weigh 130 lbs, or 117 lbs at the lower end if she is petite or 143 lbs if she is muscular. (1.7 m; 59 kg, 53-65 kg)

Men: 106 pounds (48 kg) for the first 5 feet (1.52 m) of height;
6 pounds (2.7 kg) per inch (2.5 cm) thereafter

Example: A man who is 5'10" could appropriately weigh 166 lbs, or 150 lbs at the lower end if he is petite or 182 lbs if he is muscular. (1.8 m; 75.5 kg, 68-83 kg)

If you are striving to weigh significantly less than the weight estimated by these general guidelines, think again. Remember: in addition to skill, soccer is a game of strength, endurance and power. In addition to the genetic design for your body, if you are a serious player, your soccer training, as well as the conditioning (including weights) is meant to increase performance and prevent injury. It is also likely to create a muscular body. The best weight goal is the weight that makes you feel strong and powerful. That's the "body beautiful," and the body for performance and health!

If you are wasting your time and energy complaining or worrying about your body, take a deep breath and relax. Life is a gift, too short to be spent obsessing about food and weight. Be appreciative of all your body can do for you—such as play "the beautiful game"—and stop criticizing your body for what it is not.

You can be fit, healthy, and happy at any size. You can also be miserable at your "perfect weight" if the cost of attaining that weight is yo-yo dieting, poor nutrition, lack of energy to exercise, guilt for eating, and a sense of failure that crushes your self-esteem. Then, no weight will be good enough to create happiness. So, eat well, play well, and be well.

A Note to Parents

Many young players succumb to the stereotypical female quest for a thin body; they constantly talk about dieting. Others are quieter about weight concerns, but you can easily notice they aren't eating enough. Active involvement in soccer helps many dieters realize the best players are almost never involved with unreasonable dieting—it's contrary to their goals. These serious players are too busy fueling appropriately to get better at their game.

With time comes acceptance; the maturing players replace the drive to be thin-at-any price with appreciation of the body as being their vehicle to success. One beauty of being involved in soccer (and any sports) is that the athletes learn to appreciate all the wonderful things their bodies do for them. Women's Professional Soccer is a great vehicle to emphasize this appreciation!

Summary

Food is fuel. You need to fuel your muscles appropriately even if you are trying to lose weight. Be realistic about your expectations and remember being "thin for thin's sake" does not equate to good soccer performance. Also, keep in mind the following keys to successful weight control:

1. Cut back only 100 to 300 calories a day; don't starve yourself.
2. Fuel during the day, and then eat a little less at night. If you wake up ready for breakfast, you have likely lost body fat overnight, while you were sleeping.
3. Include a little bit of (healthful) dietary fat at each meal to keep you from feeling hungry and also from feeling denied tasty foods.
4. Strive to maintain weight if you get injured or during the off-season; that's easier than losing weight during the season.
5. Honor your genetics and be realistic with your weight goals.
6. Win with good nutrition!

For more information:
http://www.cdc.gov/nccdphp/dnpa/healthyweight/

This website, sponsored by the Centers for Disease Control, offers abundant information on how to lose weight by eating well. You'll find information on calories, meal planning, exercise, and weight reduction tips for the long run.

Chapter 17
Dieting Gone Awry

Too many soccer players (mostly female players) feel pressure to lose weight. They've been led to believe "thinner is better." But that's not true in this game. Some of these players strive to be "perfectly" thin and they commonly pay a high price: poor nutrition, poorly fueled muscles, stress fractures, nagging injuries, loss of menses (in females), to say nothing of reduced stamina, endurance, and performance. For some, obsessions with food and weight culminate in disordered eating patterns, if not outright eating disorders. If you struggle with food, keep reading!

"It doesn't matter whether you are a man or a woman, muscles are cool. The better you fuel your body, the more powerful you'll be, and that's what you need for getting to the next level."

Abby Wambach, Washington Freedom forward and U.S. National Team star, who at 5'10" 160 Ibs. says she has never had trouble with her body image.

Soccer Players and Weight

Weight tends to be a major issue among some soccer players, like it is with many women. Sometimes these players are overfat and rightfully discontent with their undesired flab. Other times, they are actually lean and simply have distorted body images.

The Madison Avenue image that adorns every storefront and magazine ad leads us to believe that Nature makes all people universally lean. Wrong! Nature makes us in different sizes and shapes. If you are a female, remember: Body fat is necessary to protect your ability to create and nourish healthy babies and to provide a storehouse of calories for pregnancy and breast-feeding. This essential body fat is stored not only in the breasts but also in the hips, abdomen, and upper legs. But counter to Nature's plan, some women deem this fat as being undesirable.

Whereas 11 to 13% of a woman's body weight is essential fat stores, only 3 to 5% of a man's body weight is essential body fat. Hence, women who try to achieve the "cut look" of male athletes commonly have to starve themselves—and end up obsessing about food as they struggle to reach an unnatural image.

If you are training harder and harder to lose body fat, stop! You should train to enhance performance, not to reshape your body. Exercise as punishment for having excess body fat is not sustainable, and commonly results in injuries. If all athletes who are discontent with their weight could only learn to appreciate and love their bodies as being "good enough," eating disorders would be rare among them.

BODY IMAGE

You often hear female soccer players complain, "My thighs are so big…" Yet, a female player feels complimented if you comment her thighs are thin—even if that thinness does not benefit her performance. In contrast, you'll never hear a guy compliment his teammate by saying, "John, your thighs are so thin!"

As the legendary women's soccer coach Anson Dorrance laments, "Why do boys want to be big and powerful and rule the Earth, while girls want to be thin and small?" You can help break this cycle. Understand that the beauty of your game, and your body, is that it is about being "big and powerful and ruling the field." Women's Professional Soccer role models serve an excellent function in this way. Young girls see them up close and personal—and none of them who reach this level looks unnaturally thin or frail. They couldn't get to be pros if they were.

Women, Soccer, and Amenorrhea

If you are a female who previously had regular menstrual periods but currently has stopped menstruating, you are experiencing amenorrhea. Amenorrhea is defined as missing three or more periods in a row (as opposed to occasionally missing a period or having irregular cycles). Although you may think the loss of menses is because you are too thin or are exercising too much, thinness and exercise are generally not the causes of amenorrhea. After all, many thin soccer players do have regular menses.

Why then, given a group of females who have a similar training program and the same low percent of body fat, do some experience menstrual problems while others don't? Some players are naturally thin, but the players with amenorrhea generally have to undereat to maintain their desired weight. The cost of achieving this desired leanness is inadequate calories and, consequently, loss of menses. If the amenorrhea is caused by very restrictive eating, it can be a symptom of pain and unhappiness in your life.

Hence, athletic amenorrhea tends to be a nutritional problem and sometimes is a red flag for an eating disorder. If you stop having regular menstrual periods, be sure to consult with both your gynecologist and a sports nutritionist for professional guidance.

Health risks associated with amenorrhea

You may deem amenorrhea a desirable side effect of exercise because you no longer have to deal with the hassles and possible discomfort of monthly menstrual periods. Yet, amenorrhea can lead to undesirable problems that can interfere with your health and ability to perform at your best. These problems include:

- almost a three-time higher incidence of stress fractures.
- premature osteoporosis (weakening of the bones) that can affect your bone health in the not-too-distant as well as far future.
- inability to conceive should you want to have a baby and difficulty conceiving once you regain regular menses.

Note that the "absence of at least three consecutive menstrual cycles" is also part of the American Psychiatric Association's definition for anorexia.

Amenorrheic females who resume menses can restore some of the bone density lost during their months of amenorrhea, particularly if they are younger than seventeen years. But they do not restore all of it. Your goal should be to minimize the damages of amenorrhea by eating appropriately and taking the proper steps to regain your menstrual periods.

Resolving amenorrhea

The possible changes required to resume menses include:

- training 5 to 15% less (e.g. 50 minutes instead of an hour).
- consuming 10% more calories each week, until you ingest an appropriate amount given your activity level. To allay the "fear of eating," and get used to a more normal routine, try incremental increases. For example, if you have been eating 1,000 calories a day, eat 100 more calories per day for a total of 1,100 total calories a day during the first week (or even for 2 to 3 days); eat a total of 1,200 calories per day the second week; 1,300 the third week, and so on. (See Chapter 14 for how to determine an appropriate calorie intake.)

Some amenorrheic athletes have resumed menses with just reduced exercise and no weight gain. Others resume menstruating after gaining fewer than five pounds (that is, rebuilding and restoring five pounds of health). And despite what you may think, this small amount of weight gain tends to include muscle-gain and does not result in "getting fat."

How to Build a Better Food Plan

If you maintain your body weight despite eating minimal calories and are spending too much time thinking about food, here's a sample food plan to help you begin to fuel your body better. Gradually add 100 calories every 3 to 7 days (or every day, for that matter) and observe the benefits: you will likely feel stronger, happier, warmer; sleep better; have better workouts, and think less about food. Because you are adding essential (not excess) calories to get your body out of hibernation, you will be unlikely to "get fat." Your best bet to help you through this process of relearning how to eat appropriately is to go to www.eatright.org or www.SCANdpg.org and use the referral networks to find a local sports dietitian who can provide personalized advice.

Baseline Menu: 1,000 calories	How to increase by +100 calories/week x 8 weeks	Improved 1,800-calorie Menu	
Breakfast Special K, 1 cup (30 g) 100	Week #1. Add banana: +100	Special K, 2 cups	200
	Week #5. Add 100 cals more cereal	Banana	100
Milk, 1/2 cup 50		Milk, 1/2 cup	50
Apple, average 100		Apple	100
	Week #6. Add 14 almonds: +100	Almonds, 14	100
Lunch Salad 100		Salad	100
Tuna, small can 100	Week #2. Larger can tuna: +100	Tuna, large can	200
	Week #3. Add 1 cup yogurt: +100	Yogurt, 1 cup	100
	Week #7. Add crackers: +100	Crackers	100
Snack Energy bar 250		Energy bar	250
Dinner Chicken breast, 4 oz 200		Chicken breast	200
Broccoli, 2 cups 100		Broccoli, 2 cups	100
	Week #4. Add 1/2 cup rice: +100 cals	Rice, 1/2 cup	100
	Week #8. Add 1 cup milk: +100 cals	Milk, 1 cup	100
Total: 1,000 calories			1,800

Steps to Resolve Eating Disorders

If you are spending too much time obsessing about food, weight and exercise, seek help and information on these websites:

National Eating Disorders Association (information and referral network)
www.NationalEatingDisorders.org

American Dietetic Association (referral network)
www.eatright.org

Something Fishy Website on Eating Disorders (information and referral network)
www.something-fishy.org

Gurze Books (recommended self-help books)
www.bulimia.com

It's simply an unfortunate fact that eating disorders are a part of women's soccer, like many women's sports and women's lives. If you suspect your teammate(s) or friend is struggling with food issues, speak up! Anorexia and bulimia are self-destructive eating behaviors that may signal underlying depression and can be life-threatening. Here are some helpful tips:

- Approach the person gently but be persistent. Say that you are worried about her health. She, too, may be concerned about her loss of concentration, light-headedness, or chronic fatigue. These health changes are more likely to be a stepping-stone to accepting help, since the person clings to food and exercise for feelings of control and stability. If you are a parent, pay attention to your own player's eating habits, and those of her teammates. Consult with other parents or the coach if necessary.
- Don't discuss weight or eating habits. Address the fundamental problems of life. Focus on unhappiness as the reason for seeking help. Point out how anxious, tired, and/or irritable the person has been lately or, how unhappy she is with her performance on the field. Emphasize that she doesn't have to be that way.
- Suggest the coach or team manager distribute or post a list of resources (with tear-off websites at the bottom) where the person will see it (see resources listed above).

Be proactive. Invite a sports nutritionist or other eating disorders expert to give a talk to the team.

Remember that you are not responsible and can only try to help. Your power comes from connecting with community resources and health professionals, such as a counselor, nutritionist, or eating disorders clinic.

The following tips may help you resume menses or at least rule out nutrition-related factors.

1. *Throw away the bathroom scale.* Rather than striving to achieve a certain number on the scale, let your body weigh what it weighs. Focus on how healthy you feel and how well you perform, rather than on the number of pounds you weigh.

2. *If you have weight to lose, don't crash-diet but rather moderately cut back on your food intake by about 20%.* Rapid weight loss may predispose you to amenorrhea. By following a healthy reducing program, such as outlined in Chapter 16, you'll not only have greater success with long-term weight loss, but also have enough energy to play well. Research suggests you need to eat at least 13.5 calories per pound (30 cals/kg) that you do not burn off. That means 1,600 calories for a 120 lb (55 kg) person plus additional calories for playing soccer.

3. *If you are at an appropriate weight, practice eating as you did as a child.* Eat when you are hungry, stop when you are content. If you are always hungry and are constantly obsessing about food, you are undoubtedly trying to eat too few calories. Chapter 14 can help you determine an appropriate calorie intake and eating schedule that may differ from your current routine, particularly if you yo-yo between starving and bingeing.

4. *Eat adequate protein.* Research has suggested that amenorrheic athletes tend to eat less protein than their regularly menstruating counterparts. Even if you are a vegetarian, remember that you still need adequate protein (see Chapter 6).

5. *Eat at least 20% of your calories from fat.* Some soccer players are afraid of eating fat, thinking if they eat fat, they'll get fat. Although excess calories from fat are easily fattening, some fat (20 to 30% of total calories) is an appropriate part of a healthy sports diet, especially healthy fats. (See Chapter 7.)

6. *Maintain a calcium-rich diet to help maintain bone density.* Because females build peak bone density in their teens and early adult years, the goal is to protect against future problems with osteoporosis by including a serving of milk, yogurt, and other dairy or calcium-rich foods at each meal in the day. An adequate target is at least 1,000 milligrams of calcium per day if you are between 19 and 50 years old, and 1,200 to 1,500 milligrams of calcium per day if you are an amenorrheic or post-menopausal woman or a man over 50 years old.

Summary

Food should be one of life's pleasures, a fun part of your soccer program, and a protector of your good health. If you spend too much time thinking about food as being a fattening enemy, we highly recommend you consult with a registered dietitian who specializes in sports nutrition and eating disorders (Use the referral network at www.SCANdpg.org). This professional can help you transform your food fears into healthful fueling, so your body can support your athletic goals with good health, high energy, and positive feelings towards food and your body.

WINNING RECIPES:
Eating with a Purpose

This is a collection of favorite recipes from various players on the seven founding franchises of Women's Professional Soccer. Players express their pleasure on preparing and eating them. We are confident the winning formula they represent for the players will be the same for you!

The vast majority of recipes include a variety of "superfoods"—for soccer players and for their health-minded families and fans. (A few recipes fit into the "occasional treat" category.) The recipes are unique dishes and baked goods with good nutrition, good taste and a track record of contributing to soccer success and celebrating sports accomplishments. (Many of the recipes have been eaten before and after winning major games and championships!).

The league, as well as each of the nine teams as of 2010, is proudly represented by a signature recipe below. These recipes emphasize the many ingredients endorsed in the book, and are historically great team and family pleasers. They are also comprised of the foods that many Women's Professional Soccer players enjoy on a regular basis.

"Fueling my body with healthy food is just as important as making sure I do ball work and fitness training. Eating wisely is part of taking my game to the next level."

Kendall Fletcher, Midfielder, Saint Louis Athletica

BREAKFASTS
Manya Makoski's Snickerdoodle Pancakes
Karina LeBlanc's Game Day Pancakes
Nikki Krzysik's and Lydia Williams' Soufflé Omelet
Christie Rampone's Carrot Apple Muffins
FC Gold Pride Good Grain Granola
Sky Blueberry FC French Toast

SMOOTHIES & MUNCHIES
Cori Alexander's Strawberry Banana Smoothie
Nicole Barnhart's Peanut Butter Smoothie
Natalie Spilger's Pick-Me-Up Trail Mix
Wozzie's Wild Guacamole
Boston Breakers Black Bean Spinach Dip

SOUPS, STEWS, CHILI
Christie Welsh's Chicken Noodle Soup
Karina LeBlanc's Chicken Stew
Aly Wagner's Turkey Chili
Kacey White's Grandmother's Shrimp Gumbo
Rosana's Feijoada

SIDE DISHES
Brandi Chastain's Avocado Salad
Stephanie Cox's Tossed Salad with Cranberries and Pecans
Cat Whitehill's Sweet Potato Fries
Rachel Buehler's Easy Party Chicken Wings
Atlanta Beat Tomato Casserole
Heather O'Reilly's Herb Baked Potatoes
Chicago Red Stars Noodle Pudding
Saint Louis Athletica Quinoa Salad

MAIN MEALS
Carli Lloyd's Vegetable Quiche
Kristine Lilly's Chicken with Mushrooms and Roasted Potatoes
Val Henderson's Braised Moroccan Chicken
Kristine Lilly's Pasta with Chicken
Keeley Dowling's Barbeque Salmon
Homare Sawa's Sushi
Nancy Augustyniak Goffi's Enchilada Casserole
Marta's Signature Lasagna
Brittany Bock's Brats
Sophia Perez's Burgers with a Difference
Tasha Kai's Favorite Fried Rice
Aya Miyama's Japanese-style Hamburgers
Philadelphia Independence Bagel Panini
Los Angeles Sol Mexican Pizza

SWEETS AND TREATS
Abby Wambach's Date Bars
Allison Falk's Black Bottom Cupcakes
Washington Freedom Peanut Butter Cereal Bars
Women's Professional Soccer Apple Snack Cake

Manya Makoski's Snickerdoodle Pancakes

This is a breakfast version of the classic Snickerdoodle cookie from Manya Makoski, Midfielder, Los Angeles Sol. Manya's addition of yogurt and strawberries makes this a complete and healthful meal.

2 eggs
1/4 cup (35 g) sugar
2 teaspoons (10 g) baking powder
1/4 teaspoon (1 g) salt
2 teaspoons (10 g) vanilla extract
2 teaspoons (2 g) ground cinnamon
2 cups (250 g) flour (preferably half whole wheat)
1/2 cup (120 ml) milk

1. Beat eggs and sugar together with a whisk.

2. Add in the baking powder, salt, vanilla, and cinnamon. Gently stir the flour and milk until the batter is mixed well.

3. Heat the frying pan and spray with non-stick cooking spray. Pour batter into small circles on the frying pan. Flip when small bubbles reach the surface of the batter and the edges of the pancakes are dry.

4. Enjoy with vanilla yogurt and strawberries.

Yield: 4 servings
Total Calories: 1,200 (without toppings)
Calories per serving: 300

60 g Carbohydrate
9 g Protein
3 g Fat

Karina LeBlanc's Game Day Pancakes

Los Angeles Sol Goalkeeper Karina LeBlanc enjoys these pancakes the morning before every home game. As she simply says, "Yummy!"

Per serving:
$^2/_3$ cup (80 g) pancake mix
1 teaspoon (2 g) cinnamon

1 cup (200 g) diced fruit
(strawberries/blueberries/cantaloupe/pineapple/bananas)
1 6-ounce-cup (180 g) vanilla yogurt
2 tablespoons (40 g) maple syrup

1. Follow the directions on the pancake mix box and add 1 teaspoon of cinnamon per serving to the mix.

2. Cook the pancakes on a hot griddle, then stack on a plate.

3. Top with chopped fruit, then vanilla yogurt, and maple syrup.

4. As Karina suggests, "Open your mouth and be ready to taste greatness!"

Yield: 1 hearty serving
Total Calories: 650
Calories per serving: 650

134 g Carbohydrate
15 g Protein
6 g Fat

Nikki Krzysik's and Lydia Williams' Soufflé Omelet

Says Philadelphia Independence Defender Nikki Krzysik, who makes this recipe with Goalkeeper and roommate Lydia Williams, "This is our favorite game day recipe. Lydia has to break and separate the eggs because I always get shells in the bowl, but I whisk them. We equally share the cutting responsibility and alternate the filling of the omelet each week. Except when we are on a winning streak, then we keep the fillings the same. This is a great and easy breakfast that is so delicious." Boost the meal's carb content by having a big glass of orange juice and a bagel or toast, and then enjoy a winning day!

Per serving:
2 eggs
Salt and pepper, as desired

Filling: Whatever combination of meats, veggies and cheese you desire, such as—
2 ounces (60 g) ham, diced
$^1/_2$ to 1 cup (20 to 80 g) vegetables, such as sliced mushrooms and baby spinach
$^1/_4$ cup (1 ounce) grated cheese, preferably low-fat

1. Break eggs and separate the egg yolks from the egg whites, putting each into two small bowls.
2. In the egg yolk mixture, whisk in some salt and pepper to taste and add the ham and vegetables. (You can pre-cook these additions, if desired.)
3. Whisk the egg whites until stiff; then fold the egg yolk mixture into the egg white mixture.
4. Heat an oven-proof frying pan with cooking oil spray or butter and pour in omelet mixture. Cook over medium heat for 2 to 3 minutes.
5. Sprinkle on cheese and then place the omelet (in the pan) under a preheated broiler and broil for 3 to 4 minutes or until the cheese is golden and bubbling.
6. Fold over omelet and serve onto a plate.

Yield: 1 omelet
Total Calories: 300 (made with cooking spray)
Calories per serving: 300

6 g Carbohydrate
29 g Protein
18 g Fat

Christie Rampone's Carrot Apple Muffins

Relates Christie, 2009 player/coach of WPS Championship Sky Blue FC and captain of the U.S. National Team, "My role model growing up was my mom's best friend Jo Eckert ("Ma Eckert"). She would cook all kinds of dishes—including baking muffins—for all my teams. I always wanted to be like her, especially for my 4-year-old Rylie and her friends. Rylie has a million questions for me while I am baking so I feel like she already has the basic idea. If she ends up playing sports, I want to be known as the mom who cooks and bakes good food for the team to eat."

These hearty, health-filled muffins are moist without fat (oil or butter), and are a nice alternative to commercial sports bars. Fill muffin cups fairly high, since the apples and carrots cook down, and the muffins don't rise high. You can eat these as they are, or with peanut or almond butter.
(To make oat flour, which is delicious in this recipe, put raw rolled oats in the blender or food processor and grind until fine.)

1$^1/_2$ cups (190 g) flour	$^3/_4$ cup (180 ml) milk
1$^1/_2$ cups (140 g) oat bran or oat flour (or replace some with ground flax seed)	2 eggs, beaten
	1/2 tablespoon (7 g) vanilla
$^1/_2$ cup (95 g) brown sugar, packed	1$^1/_2$ cups (100 g) shredded carrots
2 teaspoons (10 g) baking powder	1$^1/_2$ apples (300 g) peeled and shredded
2 teaspoons (10 g) baking soda	$^1/_2$ cup (70 g) raisins
$^1/_2$ teaspoon (3 g) salt	
2 teaspoons (5 g) cinnamon	

Optional: 1 cup (120 g) chopped walnuts

1. In a medium bowl, mix flour, oat bran, brown sugar, baking powder, baking soda, salt and cinnamon.
2. Add the beaten eggs, vanilla and milk, then the carrots, apples, raisins and nuts. Stir gently until blended.
3. Prepare muffin tins with paper cups (treated with cooking spray for best results) or cooking spray. Fill the muffin cups.
4. Bake in preheated oven at 350° F (180° C) for 15-20 minutes. Test for doneness with a toothpick.

Yield: 18 muffins
Total Calories: 2,250
Calories per serving: 125

25 g Carbohydrate
4 g Protein
1 g Fat

FC Gold Pride Good Grain Granola

California—specifically the Bay Area, home of FC Gold Pride—popularized granola. Here's a new twist—a cross between granola and muesli, a healthy European cereal based on uncooked rolled oats. The wholesome ingredients in this recipe pack a nutritional punch on every level. The quinoa and millet (available in whole foods markets and many supermarkets) take on the crunchy consistency of nuts. However, they can be replaced with more oats, nuts or seeds. If you like a sweeter granola, add more dried fruit.

1 cup (180 g) dates, chopped	1 tablespoon (7 g) cinnamon, or more to taste
1 cup water	$1/2$ cup (110 g) vegetable oil, preferably canola
7 cups (560 g) rolled oats, uncooked	
$1/2$ cup (90 g) quinoa, uncooked	$1/3$ cup (80 g) apple juice concentrate (or brown sugar)
$1/2$ cup (90 g) millet, uncooked	
$1/2$ cup (70 g) pumpkin or sunflower seed kernels	1 cup (115 g) toasted wheat germ
1 tablespoon (15 g) vanilla	1 cup (145 g) raisins, or more to taste

Optional: $1/2$ cup (70 g) walnuts, chopped apricots or other dried fruit

1. Place dates and water in a small saucepan. Cook over medium heat until most of the water is absorbed and the dates are soft. Let cool a bit, and transfer to a blender or food processor and buzz to make a thick paste.
2. Heat oven to 350° F (180° C). Combine oats, quinoa, millet, seeds and walnuts. Spread on two large cookie sheets. Toast for 7 minutes. Remove and let cool a bit.
3. Lower the oven temperature to 300 degrees.
4. In a large bowl, combine apple juice concentrate, vanilla, cinnamon, oil, then wheat germ and date paste. Blend well, until there are no date clumps and all the dry ingredients are evenly coated.
5. Return onto baking trays and bake for approximately 20 minutes, or until browned. Turn the granola often so that edges don't burn.
6. Remove from the oven. Add the raisins and other dried fruit to the mixture to soften with the cereal's heat, and then let cereal cool on the baking trays. The granola will still be somewhat soft, but it gets crunchy as it cools.
7. Store in airtight containers or even in the freezer to maintain freshness. When serving, make sure to dig to the bottom of the container to get even amounts of grains. Serve with fresh fruit or added dried fruit as desired.

Yield: 24 servings   35 g Carbohydrate
Total Calories: 6,000   8 g Protein
Calories per serving: 250   9 g Fat

Sky Blueberry FC Baked French Toast

French toast is a popular pre-game breakfast. Baking instead of pan-frying adds a pleasantly different texture. By adding the berries in the last half of baking, the fruit gets nicely heated. You can also simply top the finished product with fresh berries or other fruit.

1 tablespoon (15 g) butter or soft tub margarine
1 tablespoon (15 g) sugar
$1/_2$ teaspoon (1 g) cinnamon
2 eggs
$1/_4$ cup (180 ml) milk
4 slices hearty bread (about 100 calories/slice; works best with thick sliced bread)
1 cup (250 g) blueberries (or other seasonal fruit)

Maple syrup, as desired

1. Preheat oven to 425° F (220° C).
2. Melt butter in a baking dish (about 9" x 13").
3. In a small bowl, mix the sugar and cinnamon; sprinkle it over the melted butter.
4. In another small bowl, beat the eggs with milk. Dip each slice of bread into the egg mixture and place into pan.
5. Distribute any extra egg mixture onto the top of bread.
6. Bake for 15 to 20 minutes, turning once after 10 minutes, or when bottom is toasted brown. (Thinner bread requires less cooking time.)
7. Sprinkle the blueberries on top of the bread for the final half of cooking.
8. Serve with maple syrup.

Yield: 2 servings
Total Calories: 950 (with 2 tablespoons maple syrup)
Calories per serving: 475

73 g Carbohydrate
15 g Protein
14 g Fat

Cori Alexander's Strawberry Banana Smoothie

Smoothies are good for meals or post-game/practice recovery drinks. Sky Blue FC Goalkeeper Cori Alexander quenches her thirst and her appetite with this recipe. Cori favors a small, portable drink blender to make smoothies anywhere she goes.

If you make this with strawberry yogurt (as opposed to strawberry banana yogurt), add one whole banana rather than half. Using frozen fruit makes a thicker and frostier shake.

Blend together:
1 6-ounce (180 g) container strawberry banana yogurt
6 ounces (180 ml) cranberry juice
4 strawberries, preferably frozen
$^1/_2$ banana
4 ice cubes
$^1/_4$ cup (35 g) powdered milk or whey protein powder

Yield: 1 satisfying meal-in-a-glass
Total Calories: 450
Calories per serving: 450

90 g Carbohydrate
19 g Protein
1 g Fat

Nicole Barnhart's Peanut Butter Smoothie

This protein-based shake—adapted from the type FC Gold Pride Goalkeeper Nicole Barnhart likes—makes a satisfying meal. If you want to enjoy it for a recovery shake, be sure to add a banana or some honey or other sweetener for carbs.

8 ounces (240 ml) skim milk
2 tablespoons (30 g) extra chunky peanut butter
5 ice cubes
$^1/_4$ cup (35 g) powdered milk or 1 scoop whey protein powder

Optional: 1 tablespoon (15 g) honey, 1 banana

1. Blenderize the milk, peanut butter, (honey and banana).

2. Add the ice cubes and blend until thick and frosty.

3. Enjoy!

Yield: 1 satisfying meal-in-a-glass
Total Calories: 400
Calories per serving: 400

36 g Carbohydrate
28 g Protein
16 g Fat

Soccer players like smoothies! They are particularly good when young players aren't hungry for solid food. FC Gold Pride Goalkeeper Nicole Barnhart often whips together some combination of the following for her lunch:

Fruit (strawberries, mixed berries, mango, bananas)
Peanut butter
Vanilla yogurt
Juice or soymilk
Ice

Natalie Spilger's Pick-Me-Up Trail Mix

Chicago Red Stars Defender Natalie Spilger snacks on this trail mix when she's looking for an energy boost. Gogi berries are rich in antioxidants and are reputed to boost the immune system. Natalie buys dried goji berries in the organic food section of a large grocery store; she prefers the sweetened ones. You can substitute dried cranberries, raisins, blueberries or any other dried fruit. Espresso beans offer a caffeine boost. Natalie buys the espresso beans at Trader Joe's. For children, you might want to replace the espresso beans with oat-squares cereal, pretzel rings, or another dried fruit.

1 cup (3 ounces; 90 g) dried goji berries or other dried berry
1 cup (4 ounces; 120 g) almonds, raw or roasted
$1/_2$ cup (2.5 ounces; 70 g) dark chocolate covered espresso beans

1. Combine all ingredients in a zippered baggie or air-tight container. Store it in your soccer bag for pre- or post-game snacking.

Yield: 6 servings (a handful, a scant $1/_4$ cup)
Total Calories: 1,400
Calories per serving: 235

25 g Carbohydrate
7 g Protein
12 g Fat

Wozzie's Wild Guacamole

Saint Louis Athletica Midfielder Angela Woznuk gives her recipe this clever title. Avocados are high in unsaturated fat, a healthful addition to a sports diet because of its anti-inflammatory effect. Boost the carb content of this snack by enjoying the guacamole with baked chips.

4 large avocados
$1^1/_2$ tablespoons (20 g) sour cream, preferably low-fat
$^1/_2$ tablespoon (8 ml) lemon juice
$^1/_2$ tablespoon (8 ml) lime juice
$^1/_2$ to 1 teaspoon of garlic salt, to taste
2 roma tomatoes, diced
1 medium red onion, diced
Salt to taste

1. Peel the avocados and mash with a fork in a large bowl.

2. Mix in sour cream, lemon juice and lime juice.

3. Add garlic salt and mix thoroughly.

4. Gently mix in diced tomatoes and onion.

5. If possible, refrigerate for at least 20 minutes before serving.

Yield: 10 servings
Total Calories: 2,100
Calories per serving: 210

10 g Carbohydrate
2 g Protein
18 g Fat

SMOOTHIES & MUNCHIES

173

Boston Breakers Black Bean Spinach Dip

Here's a tasty dip that's a helpful recovery food because it is rich in both carbs and protein. Bring it to a post-game tailgate party, along with some baked chips.

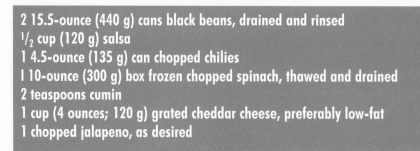

2 15.5-ounce (440 g) cans black beans, drained and rinsed
$^1/_2$ cup (120 g) salsa
1 4.5-ounce (135 g) can chopped chilies
1 10-ounce (300 g) box frozen chopped spinach, thawed and drained
2 teaspoons cumin
1 cup (4 ounces; 120 g) grated cheddar cheese, preferably low-fat
1 chopped jalapeno, as desired

Optional: $^1/_4$ cup fresh chopped cilantro, or to taste

1. Mash the beans either by hand using the back of a fork or in a blender or food processor. Leave some beans whole, for varied texture.

2. In a medium bowl, combine the beans, salsa, chilies, spinach, cumin, cheese (cilantro and jalapeno).

3. Pour the bean mixture into a pie-plate or other similar baking dish. Bake in 350° F (180° C) oven until well heated, about 20-30 minutes.

4. Serve with baked corn chips.

Yield: 10 servings
Total Calories: 1,200 (without chips)
Calories per serving: 120

16 g Carbohydrate
9 g Protein
2 g Fat

Christie Welsh's Chicken Noodle Soup

Chicken noodle soup is an easy-to-digest pre-game meal that offers fluids, sodium, carbs and protein. It's also a wonderful recovery food after a cold-weather game when players are chilled. As Saint Louis Athletica Forward Christie reports, "This is my fav!"

SOUPS, STEWS, CHILI

2 chicken breasts, with bone
3 cups (24 ounces; 720 ml) chicken broth, from bouillon cubes or canned
2 carrots, diced
2 stalks celery, diced
1 small onion, diced
2 cups (330 g) corn, frozen or canned
Salt and pepper to taste
8 ounces (240 g) pasta, uncooked (e.g. small shells, bow ties, etc.)

1. Drop two chicken breasts (bone in) into a big pot.
2. Add enough broth just to cover the chicken, about 3 cups.
3. Cover, cook until chicken is done, about 20 to 30 minutes.
4. Remove chicken, let it cool for about 10 minutes, cut or pull it off the bone, and then put the chicken back in the broth.
5. While the chicken is cooling, skim the fat off the broth.
6. Cut up the carrots, celery and onion. Add them to the broth with the chicken.
7. Cook for another 30 to 60 minutes; then add the corn.
8. While the corn is cooking, in a separate pot, cook the pasta (shape of your choice).
9. Add the cooked pasta to the soup; add more chicken broth, salt and pepper, as desired.

Yield: 5 servings (as a part of a meal)
Total Calories: 1,500
Calories per serving: 300

50 g Carbohydrate
20 g Protein
2 g Fat

Karina LeBlanc's Chicken Stew

This recipe is one of Los Angeles Sol Goalkeeper Karina's favorite chicken dishes; it has a Caribbean touch. Her mom used to cook it for her. You can simplify this recipe by tossing all the ingredients (minus the lemon) into a crock pot and let it cook for four hours. Start cooking it before an afternoon game, and dinner will be ready and waiting when you get home.

3+ pounds (1.3 kg) chicken parts, skin removed	$1/2$ cup (120 ml) cold water
$1/2$ lemon	1 tablespoon (10 g) brown sugar
2 cloves garlic, crushed	1 tablespoon (15 ml) olive oil
1 tablespoon (15 ml) white vinegar	$1 1/4$ cups (300 ml) water or chicken broth
1 teaspoon (5 g) salt	2 tablespoons (20 g) flour
$1/2$ teaspoon (1 g) thyme	1 onion, sliced
$1/2$ teaspoon (1 g) cayenne pepper	1 stalk celery, diced

Option: Add 4 potatoes, cut into chunks.

1. Wash the chicken pieces thoroughly in cold water and then rub with lemon.
2. Add crushed garlic, vinegar, salt, thyme, pepper, and $1/2$ cup of cold water to chicken in a bowl. Cover and shake well for 1 minute. Marinate in refrigerator overnight if possible. Drain the chicken.
3. Heat the brown sugar in a large skillet, over medium heat, until dark brown (melted).
4. Add the oil; mix well; then add the chicken. Stir the chicken in the skillet until covered with brown mixture. Cover and simmer over medium heat.
5. Check often to see if more water needs to be added to prevent sticking.
6. When the chicken pieces are dark brown, add $1 1/2$ cups of warm water or chicken broth to the chicken and cook until tender. Optional: Add potato chunks.
7. Make a thin paste by mixing the flour and a little warm water and then whisking it into gravy to thicken it. Lower the heat.
8. Add the sliced onion and diced celery. (You can also add other vegetables, such as mushrooms.) Simmer gently for 10-15 minutes.

Yield: 4 servings
Total Calories: 1,300
Calories per serving: 325

10 g Carbohydrate
44 g Protein
12 g Fat

Aly Wagner's Turkey Chili

A hearty bowl of chili is a welcome recovery food after a brisk fall soccer game. Here's a deliciously different chili, unlike any you have probably tasted before, from Los Angeles Sol Midfielder Aly Wagner. The secret ingredient is pineapple salsa. (Aly recommends Trader Joe's brand). Any type of fruit salsa will yield an equally tasty meal.

If you cannot find roasted diced tomatoes, simply use whatever type of canned, diced or pureed tomato product is handy.

2 pounds (1 kg) ground turkey
2 tablespoons (30 ml) oil, preferably olive or canola
1 onion
$^3/_4$ pound (12 ounces; 340 g) baby carrots
1 red pepper
1 15.5-ounce (440 g) can red kidney beans
2 28-ounce (785 g) cans of roasted, diced tomatoes
2 12-ounce (335 g) jars of pineapple salsa
$^1/_2$ teaspoon (1 g) cinnamon
1 6-ounce (170 g) can tomato paste mixed with 8 ounces of water
Salt, as desired

1. Brown the turkey in one tablespoon of oil, drain, and set aside.

2. In a mini food processor, chop up quartered onion, carrots and red pepper.
    (If you do not have a food processor, chop them finely by hand.)

3. Sauté the vegetables together in another tablespoon of olive oil.

4. Add tomatoes, salsa, and seasoning. Bring to a boil and simmer. Make sure carrots are cooked through. Add turkey and tomato paste. Cook as long as desired.

Yield: 6 hearty servings   42 g Carbohydrate
Total Calories: 2,700   37 g Protein
Calories per serving: 450   15 g Fat

Kacey White's Grandmother's Shrimp Gumbo

Gumbo is a Louisiana soup or stew. This recipe, adapted from Sky Blue FC Midfielder Kacey White's grandmother, Dorothy Skelton, is made with shrimp, but can also be made with other kinds of seafood, diced turkey or chicken.

A secret ingredient is gumbo file (pronounced fee-lay, finely ground sassafras leaves, available at some supermarkets, or on the Internet). In the absence of file, use Cajun seasonings or cayenne pepper. The okra serves as a thickening agent. To serve, put cooked rice in the bottom of a bowl, then ladle the gumbo on top.

3 tablespoons oil, preferably olive or canola
1 small onion, diced
$^1/_2$ medium green bell pepper, diced
1 stalk celery, diced
$^1/_4$ cup all purpose flour
3 cups chicken broth or water
1 14.5-ounce can diced tomatoes
2 cups chopped or sliced okra, frozen or fresh

1 pound raw, cleaned shrimp, preferably small or medium size
Salt and pepper to taste
$^1/_2$ tablespoon gumbo file or other Cajun seasonings, to taste

Cooked rice, preferably brown

1. In a large pot, sauté onions, bell pepper and celery in 1 tablespoon of oil for about 8 to 10 minutes, or until the onions are translucent. Remove into a small bowl and set aside.
2. Heat two remaining tablespoons of the oil in the pan. Using a wire wisk, mix the flour into the oil, stirring constantly until very brown. (Kacey warns to be sure to stir the flour and oil constantly so that it will not burn while flour is browning.) Cook it slowly over low heat; some patient cooks let it brown slowly for 10 to 20 minutes, until it is golden.
3. Add broth or water in small amounts into browned flour mixture, stirring constantly.
4. Add tomatoes, bring to a boil, and then add celery, onion, and bell pepper. Reduce the heat and simmer uncovered for about 20 minutes (or less, if you are impatient!), stirring occasionally.
5. Add shrimp and okra and bring to a boil; then add seasonings. Simmer for 5 minutes.
6. Preferably, let the gumbo sit for about one hour to allow the flavors to blend. Reheat and then serve over cooked, warm rice placed in the bottom of a soup bowl.

Yield: 4 servings
Total Calories: 1,200 (without rice)
Calories per serving: 300

24 g Carbohydrate
26 g Protein
11 g Fat

Rosana's Feijoada

Rosana (Brazilian players traditionally go by one name), Midfielder on Sky Blue FC, enjoys feijoada with her family on Sundays in her home in São Paulo. Feijoada, called the "national dish of Brazil," includes various types of meat and seasonings. While the traditional recipe might call for pig's feet, swine tails and beef tongue, this modernized recipe offers a delicious taste with more healthful (and readily available) ingredients. This tastes even better after a day of refrigeration. Says Rosana on eating this version, "If I close my eyes, I think I am home!"

1 medium onion, chopped
1 jalapeno pepper, whole or diced
3 tablespoons (45 ml) oil, preferably olive or canola
3 cloves garlic, minced
3 15.5-ounce (440 g) cans black beans, drained and rinsed
1 pound (450 g) chicken sausage
1 pound (450 g) sirloin, cut in pieces
$1/4$ cup (30 g) flour to coat sirloin, seasoned with paprika or other spices, if desired

$1/2$ package (6 ounces; 170 g) turkey bacon
2 to 4 bay leaves
1 teaspoon (2 g) cumin
2 cups (480 ml) beef or chicken broth (enough to cover all ingredients in pot)
1 orange, sliced

Cooked rice, preferably brown

1. Cut the onion into medium-sized pieces.

2. Heat half the oil in a large pot (cast iron is best); brown the onions and jalapeno.

3. Mince the garlic and add it at the last minute, being careful not to burn it. Remove the mixture from the pot and set aside in a medium-sized bowl.

4. Score (put slits in) the chicken sausage about one inch apart. Cook it in the pot until it is well browned on the outside (it need not be fully cooked). Remove the sausage from pot and set aside with the onions. Wipe out pot to remove any fat.

5. Put the flour in a plastic bag; add the sirloin pieces and shake to coat (or put flour on a plate to coat them.) Heat the remainder of the oil in the pot and cook the beef just until it is browned on the outside. Remove from pot and set aside in the bowl with the onions and sausage.

6. Slice the bacon in one-inch pieces. Quickly brown, about 1 to 2 minutes, then remove and set aside with the other cooked ingredients. Wipe the pot to remove any fat.

7. Drain the beans and put all ingredients into the pot. Add the jalapeno, bay leaves and cumin.

8. Pour in the broth, just to cover. Bring to a boil, cover the pot, and simmer 30 to 40 minutes, stirring occasionally.

9. Remove the cover and simmer another 20 to 30 minutes, stirring occasionally as the mixture thickens. For extra thick stew, mash some of the beans on the side of the pot while cooking.

10. Remove the bay leaves (and the jalapeno, if left whole). Serve over cooked rice with orange slices, which help cut the heat plus are a traditional addition with this dish.

Yield: 10 servings
Total calories: 3,600 (without rice)
Calories per serving: 360

25 g Carbohydrate
27 g Protein
17 g Fat

Brandi Chastain's Avocado Salad

Soccer legend Brandi Chastain, who plays Midfield in her native Bay Area with FC Gold Pride, says, "This is straight from the kitchen of my beloved mother, Lark Chastain, the greatest soccer mom, tailgate/party thrower and friend ever. It is one of my favorite, healthy, and absolutely delicious salads. This works best with avocados that are firm but with a little bit of give when you feel them. You don't want soft avocados, because they will turn into guacamole-like mush. If your tastes are like those of Kristine Lilly—who thinks cilantro tastes like soap—leave it out!"

Brandi says all portions are adjustable, taking into consideration what you like the most or how many people you are serving.

3 firm avocados, diced
1 11-ounce (310 g) can white corn or 2 ears of white corn, cooked and cut off the cob
2 roma or plum tomatoes, diced
$1/_2$ red onion, diced
1 small (or if you like it spicy, BIG) Serrano chili, diced into small bits. (Take out the seeds, or you will pay the price!)
$1/_2$ lemon, juiced, or 2 tablespoons (30 ml) lemon juice

Optional: handful of cilantro leaves, chopped; salt and pepper to taste

1. Peel and dice the avocados, tomatoes, and onion and put into a large bowl.
2. Add the corn.
3. Fold all ingredients together gently, being careful not to turn it into mush.
4. Sprinkle with lemon juice.
5. Chill for 15-20 minutes and enjoy.

Yield: 6 servings
Total Calories: 1,350
Calories per serving: 225

20 Carbohydrate
3 g Protein
15 g Fat

Stephanie Cox's Tossed Salad with Cranberries and Pecans

This recipe makes enough for the entire team—and it's a delicious way to get some vegetables (lettuces), fruit (dried cranberries), and healthful fats (olive oil and pecans). You can serve it with crusty bread, as a main meal, or enjoy it as a side dish.

$^3/_4$ cup (100 g) pecans
2 tablespoons (30 g) butter or soft tub margarine
3 tablespoons (35 g) brown sugar

1 head red leaf lettuce
1 head romaine lettuce
1 cup (150 g) dried cranberries
$^3/_4$ cup (3 ounces; 120 g) crumbled blue cheese

Dressing:
$^1/_4$ cup (60 g) olive oil
$^1/_4$ cup (60 ml) cider vinegar
2 tablespoons (30 ml) lemon juice
$^1/_4$ teaspoon (1 g) salt and pepper, as desired

Optional: 2 tablespoons (10 g) minced shallots

1. In a heavy skillet, melt the butter or margarine and brown sugar over medium heat. Add the pecans, mix well, and sauté them for several minutes, or until nicely glazed.
2. Wash and dry the lettuces; tear into pieces and place in a large salad bowl.
3. Top with cranberries, blue cheese, and glazed pecans.
4. In a small bowl, mix the oil, vinegar, (shallots), lemon juice, salt and pepper.
5. Pour the dressing over the salad and toss well.

Yield: 10 large servings   16 g Carbohydrate
Total Calories: 2,200   3 g Protein
Calories per serving: 220   16 g Fat

Cat Whitehill's Sweet Potato Fries

Here is Washington Freedom Defender Cat Whitehill's favorite recipe for sweet potato fries. Bet you can't eat just one!

2 medium (1 pound; 0.5 kg) sweet potatoes or yams
2 tablespoons (30 g) oil, olive or canola
2 tablespoons (25 g) brown sugar

1. Wash and thinly slice sweet potatoes into coin shapes.

2. Mix olive oil and brown sugar in a bowl. Add the sweet potatoes and mix well to coat the "coins."

3. Place them on a baking sheet lined with foil (for easy clean-up).

4. Bake at 425º F (220º C) degrees for about 25 to 35 minutes, or until tender. Flip them half-way through baking.

Yield: 3 servings
Total Calories: 750
Calories per serving: 250

42 g Carbohydrate
2 g Protein
8 g Fat

SIDE DISHES

Rachel Buehler's Easy Party Chicken Wings

This recipe from Rachel Buehler, Defender with FC Gold Pride, is an easy dish that the Buehlers have brought along to nearly every soccer team party over the years. Wings are higher in fat than in protein and carbs, so eat them for a treat, and be sure to accompany them with carbohydrate-rich pretzels or rolls.

4 pounds (2 kg; about 20) chicken drummettes (aka chicken wings)
$1/_2$ cup (120 ml) Kikkoman or your favorite teriyaki marinade
$1/_4$ cup (120 g) oil, preferably olive
Garlic powder and dried basil flakes, to taste

Optional: 4 plum Italian tomatoes

1. In a large plastic bag, place the drumettes, teriyaki marinade, 3 tablespoons olive oil, garlic powder and basil. Shake well until the drumettes are equally covered with the sauce.
2. Line a broiler pan with foil (for easy cleanup). Place the drumettes on the broiler tray.
3. Optional: Cut the tomatoes into lengthwise quarters. Place them around the chicken pieces. Sprinkle the tomato pieces lightly with 1 tablespoon of olive oil, a little garlic powder and dried basil flakes.
4. Place the broiler tray on a rack that is about 8 inches from the heat source. Keeping the oven door ajar, broil the chicken for about 20 to 30 minutes, turning the pieces over about every 5 to 10 minutes to avoid letting the drummettes get too burned. (Move the pan further away from the heat source, if needed, to prevent burning.)
5. When the chicken is done (the juices will run clear when pierced with a fork), place the drumettes on a pretty platter. Arrange the tomato pieces on top and enjoy!

Yield: about 20 to 30 drumettes
Total Calories: about 2,000
Calories per serving: about 100/drumette

Trace g Carbohydrate
5 g Protein
8 g Fat

Atlanta Beat Tomato Casserole

This is a delicious way to make use of an abundance of ripe tomatoes, such as in the summer when the garden overflows. This casserole is somewhat like a light pizza; in the very hot oven, the tomatoes cook down and the cheese becomes like a crust.

$1/_2$ to $3/_4$ cup (60-90 g) flour seasoned with salt, pepper, paprika, garlic powder, basil, and oregano, as desired
4-5 large tomatoes, sliced thick
2 tablespoons (30 g) oil, preferably olive
1 pound (450 g) ricotta cheese, part-skim
$1/_2$ cup (120 g) sour cream, preferably low-fat

Optional: $1/_4$ cup (10 g) chopped fresh parsley or basil

1. Preheat oven to 450° F (230° C).
2. Place flour and seasonings on a plate or in a plastic bag. Lightly coat tomato slices with flour mixture.
3. Heat the oil in a large skillet. Sauté the tomatoes in batches until browned on both sides (about 2 minutes per side). (If cooking in batches, divide oil.)
4. While the tomatoes cook, mix the ricotta, sour cream, (and parsley or basil).
5. Place tomatoes in an oiled baking dish, then top with the ricotta mixture. If you are using a smaller baking dish, place the tomato slices in layers, like lasagna, reserving enough cheese to finish and cover the top.
6. Bake for 30 to 40 minutes, or until lightly browned and bubbling.

Yield: 8 servings as a side dish
Total Calories: 1,500
Calories per serving: 185

15 g Carbohydrate
9 g Protein
10 g Fat

Heather O'Reilly's Herbed Baked Potatoes

Sky Blue FC Midfielder Heather O'Reilly's fan club is called "O'Reilly's Clan." So, from the Irish-heritage player comes a potato recipe. Baking this potato mixture in a casserole dish is far easier than re-stuffing the mixture into the skins, but you can stuff them into the skins for a nice presentation. You can also reheat any potato skins in the toaster oven until crispy. Use frozen chopped broccoli or spinach to simplify preparation.

These potatoes go nicely with steamed carrots (which players tend to devour when the carrots are coated with a little soft tub margarine or butter and honey).

4 large (10 ounces; 300 g each) baking potatoes 1 medium onion, chopped finely 2 cloves garlic, minced 1 tablespoon (15 g) oil, preferably olive or canola 2 cups (50-150 g) chopped broccoli, spinach, or other greens of choice	1/2 cup (120 ml) milk or sour cream, preferably low-fat 1-2 tablespoons (15-30 g) butter or soft tub margarine, as desired 1 cup (40 g) chopped fresh parsley 1 teaspoon (2 g) dried dill, or 2 tablespoons (1 g) fresh, chopped 1 cup (4 ounces; 120 g) strong-flavored grated cheese, such as sharp cheddar, feta, Parmesan or a mixture of them Salt and pepper, to taste

1. Bake the potatoes at 400° F (205° C) for about an hour or until soft. Let cool and scoop out the insides.
2. While the potatoes are baking, sauté the onions in oil until they are well-browned. Add the minced garlic at the last minute so it doesn't burn.
3. Mash the potatoes with milk or sour cream and butter or margarine.
4. Add the cooked onion, garlic, chopped broccoli, cheese, dill and parsley.
5. Place the potato mixture in a casserole dish that has been oiled or coated with cooking spray.
6. Bake in a preheated 350° F (180° C) oven for about 30 minutes, or until cooked hot throughout.

Yield: 8 servings　　　　43 g Carbohydrate
Total Calories: 2,100　　8 g Protein
Calories per serving: 265　7 g Fat

Chicago Red Stars Noodle Pudding

Noodle pudding—called Kugel in the Jewish tradition—is a great-tasting and performance-enhancing sports food that offers both carbs and protein. It freezes well and travels well, hence is a handy choice for post-game refueling.

This is a "no guilt" version of the traditional Kugel (which is usually brimming with butter, sugar, and full-fat versions of ingredients below). If you add extra dried fruit or pineapple, you can reduce the sugar a little bit.

1 pound (450 g) wide egg noodles
6 eggs or egg substitute
1 pound (450 g) cottage cheese, preferably low-fat or non-fat
1 cup (240 g) sour cream, preferably low-fat or non-fat
1 cup (240 g) applesauce, preferably unsweetened
$^1/_2$ cup (100 g) sugar (or slightly less if you use sweetened applesauce)
1 teaspoon (5 ml) vanilla
$^1/_2$ cup (70 g) raisins

Optional: $^1/_2$ teaspoon cinnamon; toasted wheat germ, graham cracker crumbs or crushed cornflakes for topping; chopped dried apricots, $^1/_2$ cup pineapple chunks

1. Boil the noodles for about 5 or 6 minutes or only until they are partially cooked; they will continue cooking in the oven.
2. While the noodles are cooking, in a large bowl combine the eggs, cottage cheese, sour cream, applesauce, sugar, vanilla, and raisins.
3. Add the cooked noodles, mix well, and pour into an oiled 9" x 13" baking dish.
4. Top with cinnamon and wheat germ.
5. Bake in a pre-heated 350° F (180° C) oven for 40 to 45 minutes. Test for doneness by making sure there is no liquid remaining. Be careful not to overcook the dish or it will be dry.
6. Cut in squares; serve warm or at room temperature.

Yield: 16 servings   34 g Carbohydrate
Total Calories: 3,600   11 g Protein
Calories per serving: 225   5 g Fat

Saint Louis Athletica Quinoa Salad

This colorful salad can be eaten alone, or as a side dish, and is a perfect pre- or post-soccer meal. This dish is modeled on Tabouli, a Middle Eastern classic made from bulghar wheat. Increasing the olive oil and lemon juice to 1/3 cup will create a "richer" dish. You may also consider other types of dressings, including low or non-fat, but the olive oil has great health properties. Quinoa (KEEN-wah) contains more protein than any other grain, and because it contains all the essential amino acids, it is considered a complete protein. It is a good source of dietary fiber, phosphorus, magnesium and iron. An alternative would be making this dish with couscous.

$1^1/_2$ cups (270 g) quinoa, uncooked
3 cups (720 ml) chicken or vegetable broth
1 15.5-ounce (440 g) can garbanzo beans, drained and rinsed
1 large carrot, grated
$^1/_2$ cup (70 g) dried cranberries or raisins
$^1/_2$ cup (10 g) chopped parsley
$^1/_4$ cup (60 ml) lemon juice (1 fresh lemon)
$^1/_4$ cup (60 ml) olive oil
$^1/_2$ teaspoon (2 g) salt or to taste (depending on salt content of cooking broth)

Optional additions: steamed asparagus or broccoli; chopped toasted walnuts or other nuts

1. In a large skillet under low heat on stovetop, cook the dry quinoa in a pan until just lightly toasted, stirring constantly.
2. Add 3 cups chicken or vegetable broth. Bring to a boil, lower heat, cover tightly and simmer until liquid is absorbed (15-20 minutes).
3. Add the raisins or cranberries. Cover and let steam for a few minutes to soften the dried fruit.
4. Remove the cover and let cool.
5. Put cooked quinoa in a bowl. Add the parsley, lemon juice and olive oil (and any other optional ingredients). Chill in refrigerator to allow flavors to blend.

Yield: 10 servings   33 g Carbohydrate
Total Calories: 2,200   6 g Protein
Calories per serving: 220   7 g Fat

Carli Lloyd's Vegetable Quiche

Carli Lloyd, Midfielder for Sky Blue FC, is a fan of quiche. This recipe is adapted from one of her favorites. The nutritional issue with quiche is that more than half the calories come from the fat in the crust. A crustless quiche solves that problem, and also simplifies preparation. If you make the quiche without a crust, use an oiled pie plate and serve with a bagel, rice or potatoes for a carbohydrate boost.

1 9-inch unbaked pastry shell
1 cup (160 g) diced onion
1 medium pepper, diced
1 small zucchini, diced
3 medium mushrooms, sliced
2 tablespoons (30 g) olive oil
$1/_4$ teaspoon (0.5 g) basil
$1/_4$ teaspoon (0.5 g) oregano

$1/_2$ teaspoon (1 g) salt, as desired
$1/_4$ teaspoon (0.5 g) pepper, as desired
3 eggs
$1/_2$ cup (120 ml) milk
$1/_2$ cup (2 ounces; 60 g) grated cheddar cheese, preferably low-fat
1 tomato, sliced thin

1. Bake the pastry shell for 12 minutes in a preheated 350° F (180° C) oven.
2. While the shell is baking, in a large skillet sauté the onion, pepper, zucchini and mushrooms in oil for about 5 minutes, or until tender.
3. Drain any extra liquid, and then add the basil, oregano, salt, and pepper. Mix well and then spoon it into crust.
4. In a bowl, beat together the eggs and milk. Carefully pour the egg mixture over the vegetables. Top with the tomato slices, and lastly, the grated cheese.
5. Bake at 350° F (180° C) for 40 to 45 minutes or until a knife inserted near the center comes out clean.
6. Let stand for 5 minutes before serving.

Yield: 4 servings
Total Calories: 1,750 with crust, 860 calories without crust
Calories per serving: 435 with crust, 215 without crust

with crust
36 g Carbohydrate
12 g Protein
27 g Fat

without crust
15 g Carbohydrate
10 g Protein
13 g Fat

Kristine Lilly's Chicken with Mushrooms and Roasted Potatoes

This recipe is adapted from Boston Breakers Midfielder Kristine Lilly. In order to maximally marinate the chicken overnight, you need to plan ahead. If you fail to plan ahead, simply marinate the chicken for as little as 20 minutes.

2 chicken breasts, boneless, skinless (12 ounces raw; 0.65 kg)
Italian dressing (Christine prefers Kraft)
4 red potatoes, medium-sized (7 ounces (200 g) each, uncooked)
8 mushrooms
1 tablespoon (15 g) olive oil
$^1/_2$ tablespoon (2 g) tarragon
Salt and pepper, as desired

1. Ideally, marinate the chicken breast overnight in Italian dressing.
2. Cut the potatoes into small, bite-sized pieces. Put them in a plastic bag.
3. Add one tablespoon of olive oil to the bag of potatoes. Then sprinkle in the tarragon, salt, and pepper.
4. Clean the mushrooms, trim the ends; add to the bag and shake well.
5. Heat a large non-stick frying pan, add the potatoes and mushrooms. Cover and cook over medium high heat for about 10 minutes.
6. At 10 minutes, push aside some of the potatoes to make space for the chicken. Add the chicken breasts, cover and cook along with the potatoes for 10 to 20 more minutes, or until done. Alternatively, grill the chicken and add to the cooked potatoes.

Yield: 2 servings
Total Calories: 1,200
Calories per serving: 600

75 g Carbohydrate
46 g Protein
14 g Fat

Val Henderson's Braised Moroccan Chicken

You can either make this dish the way that Philadelphia Independence Goalkeeper Val does, by browning the chicken as described below. Or, you can more simply toss all the ingredients into a crock pot so dinner can cook while you're at a soccer game or practice.

Instead of cooking the rice separately, cook it in the sauce, along with the chicken. This gives it great taste, and soaks up the extra liquid. If you make this meal ahead of time, the flavors will taste even better after all the spices really set in.

6 (1 kg) chicken thighs, preferably skinless	2 teaspoons (3 g) ginger
	Salt, pepper as desired
1 to 2 tablespoons oil (15-30 g), preferably olive or canola	1 14.5-ounce (410 g) can of chicken broth
1 onion, preferably red, diced	$1^1/_2$ (360 ml) cups orange juice (or apple juice)
4 cloves of garlic, diced	$^1/_2$ cup (70 g) dried apricots or dates mixture)
4 to 5 carrots, diced	
2 teaspoons (3 g) cinnamon	Optional: 1 cup uncooked rice

1. Heat the oil in a large skillet.
2. Sprinkle the chicken with salt and pepper.
3. When the oil is hot, place the chicken in the pan and brown it on both sides, about 5 to 6 minutes per side. Remove the chicken to a plate.
4. Remove all but about 2 tablespoons of the oil/chicken fat from the pan and heat until it is hot. Add the onion, garlic and carrots. Cover, and cook until tender, about 8 to 10 minutes, stirring every few minutes.
5. Add the cinnamon and ginger. Continue to cook for another 3 to 4 minutes.
6. Add the chicken broth and orange juice. Return chicken to the pan; add 1/2 cup of either dried apricots or dates.
7. Bring to a boil, then cook on low heat for 20 to 30 minutes, covered.
8. Optional: Add 1 cup uncooked rice to the sauce, cover, and let cook.
9. If you do not cook the rice in the sauce: Remove the cooked chicken and veggies to a dish; continue boiling the sauce until it has thickened, about another 10 minutes. (The sauce doesn't get very thick.)
10. Serve chicken over brown rice, and spoon sauce on top.

Yield: 3 servings
Total Calories: 1,450
Calories per serving: 480

40 g Carbohydrate
46 g Protein
15 g Fat

Kristine Lilly's Pasta with Chicken

Since giving birth to daughter Sidney Marie in July, 2008, legendary Boston Breakers Midfielder Kristine Lilly—the world's all-time caps (caps are international playing appearances) leader (man or woman) with 300—has surely made her busy lifestyle run more smoothly with easy dishes like the one below, and her previous chicken recipe in this section. For a complete meal, serve this with your choice of steamed vegetables.

1 chicken breast (6 ounces (170 g) before cooking), marinated in Italian dressing
3 ounces (200g) uncooked pasta, such as ziti
$^1/_2$ tablespoon (7 g) olive oil, butter or soft tub margarine
2 tablespoons (15 g) Parmesan cheese, preferably freshly grated

1. Cook the pasta according to the directions on the box.

2. While the pasta is cooking, sauté the chicken breast in a skillet over medium heat.

3. When the pasta is done, drain, put on a plate, toss with olive oil, and sprinkle with Parmesan cheese.

4. Serve with chicken (and steamed vegetables).

Yield: 1 hefty serving
Total Calories: 600
Calories per serving: 600

63 g Carbohydrate
55 g Protein
15 g Fat

Keeley Dowling's Barbeque Salmon

When Sky Blue FC Defender Keeley Dowling worked at a sports complex in Tempe, Arizona, the chef cooked this recipe. That chef taught Keeley to cover the entire piece of salmon with barbeque sauce, so it completely blankets the fish; the thicker the better! Keeley strongly recommends Sweet Baby Ray's Original BBQ Sauce. It blends very nicely with the salmon, so much so that folks who normally don't like fish will enjoy this meal. This recipe goes nicely with asparagus and rice, preferably brown.

$1/_2$ to 1 cup (120 to 240 mg or more, if desired) Sweet Baby Ray's Original BBQ Sauce
1 pound (0.5 kg) salmon

1. Preheat oven to 400° F (205° C).
2. Place salmon in a baking dish lined with foil (to simplify clean-up).
3. Cover the salmon entirely with Sweet Baby Ray's Original BBQ Sauce.
4. Bake uncovered for 20-25 minutes The fish is done when it flakes easily with a fork.

Yield: 3 servings
Total calories: 900
Calories per serving: 300

23 g Carbohydrate
30 g Protein
10 g Fat

Homare Sawa's Sushi

Homare Sawa, Midfielder for the Washington Freedom, prefers her native Japanese food, even far from home. "It is much healthier," she says, comparing it to standard American fare. Early in the 2009 WPS season, she hosted her first "sushi party," with her host family's youth soccer team and 12 of her Freedom teammates. She single-handedly made sushi for the 20 to 30 people in attendance.
Try your own post-game sushi party. It sure works for Homare Sawa, acknowledged as one of the best players in the world.

For information on how to make your own sushi: http://www.asianartmall.com/SushiSushi.html.

Nancy Augustyniak Goffi's Enchilada Casserole

Nancy, a Defender for the Boston Breakers, is a health-conscious athlete who does her "homework" on the cooking front. She likes to draw from a variety of resources, including *Cooking Light* magazine, from which this recipe has been adapted—adding even more great tasting and healthy options. It is especially good when served with avocado slices with a splash of lime.

1 cup (4 ounces; 120 g) shredded reduced-fat Monterey Jack or cheddar cheese, divided
1 cup (175 g) cooked rice (preferably brown)
1 cup (240 g) sour cream, preferably low fat or fat free, or $1/_2$ cup sour cream mixed with $1/_2$ cup low- or non-fat plain yogurt
$1/_2$ cup (40 g) chopped fresh cilantro
$1/_3$ cup (50 g) chopped green onions
1 teaspoon (2 g) ground cumin
1 teaspoon (2 g) chili powder
1 (15.5-ounce; 440 g) can black (kidney or pinto) beans, rinsed and drained
2 10-ounce (280 g) cans red enchilada sauce
12 6-inch corn tortillas

Optional: Add 2 to 3 cooked chicken breasts, diced and seasoned with cumin and chili powder, and/or 1 cup corn.

1. Preheat oven to 350° F (180° C).
2. In a medium bowl, combine 1/2 cup cheese, rice, and the rest of the ingredients through beans in a large bowl.
3. Spread $1/_4$ cup enchilada sauce in bottom of an 11" x 7" or 9" x 9" baking dish.
4. Heat the remaining sauce until warm.
5. Lightly coat both sides of 6 tortillas in the warm enchilada sauce, and arrange the tortillas, overlapping, over sauce in the baking dish. Top with $1^3/_4$ cups bean mixture. Coat and layer the remainder of the tortillas.
6. Top with the remaining bean mixture, remaining enchilada sauce, and $1/_2$ cup cheese. Bake for approximately 30 minutes or until bubbly.

Yield: 4 servings　　　　　65 g Carbohydrate
Total Calories: 1,865　　　　20 g Protein
Calories per serving: 465　　14 g Fat

Marta's Signature Lasagna

Marta, Brazilian Forward for the Los Angeles Sol and three-time FIFA World Player of the Year, admits she isn't much of a cook, but she loves this recipe because it is so simple. Marta's original recipe called for two pounds of cheese, but that creates a lasagna with only one-third of the calories from carbohydrates. Even with one pound of cheese, the lasagna gets only half its calories from carbs. The bottom line: be sure to eat extra bread, juice and fruit along with it, especially if you are trying to carbo-load for an important game.

16 lasagna noodles
1 pound (450 g) ground beef
1 48-ounce (1.3 kg) jar marinara sauce
8 ounces (225 g) mozzarella cheese, low-fat shredded
8 ounces (225 g) mild cheddar cheese, low-fat shredded

Optional: Add chopped spinach, broccoli, olives or mushrooms to the ground beef/marinara mixture.

1. Boil the lasagna noodles until almost cooked.
2. While the noodles are cooking, brown the ground beef and drain.
3. Add marinara sauce to ground beef. Set aside.
4. Mix mozzarella and cheddar cheese in a bowl.
5. Layer 9" x 13" or similar size pan in the following order: 4 lasagna noodles, ground beef/marinara mixture, (vegetables), and then the cheese mixture.
6. Repeat four times.
7. Place a piece of foil over pan of lasagna. Bake for 40 minutes at 350° F (180° C).

Yield: 10 large servings
Total Calories: 5,000
Calories per serving: 500

55g Carbohydrate
30 g Protein
18 g Fat

Brittany Bock's Brats

Los Angeles Sol Defender Brittany Bock named her own dish. Bratwurst should be an occasional treat because of its high fat content. Be sure to eat it in bulky sub rolls or with a lot of rice to boost the carbohydrate content of the meal so you can fuel your muscles and not just fill your stomach with protein and fat. A preferable alternative is turkey sausage.

4 bratwurst or turkey sausage
1 red (sweet) pepper, sliced
1 green pepper, sliced
1 small onion, diced
1-2 cloves garlic, crushed
1 tablespoon (15 g) olive oil
4 ounces (120 ml) Bock Beer

1. Grill or pan-fry the bratwurst or turkey sausages until done, about 10 minutes.

2. Meanwhile, in a large skillet, heat the olive oil and sauté the red and green peppers, onion and garlic. Cook until tender, about 10 minutes.

3. Add the beer to the peppers and onion. Simmer on low heat for about 20 minutes.

4. Combine sausages and beer/vegetable mixture and enjoy.

Yield: 4 servings
Total Calories: 1,360
Calories per serving: 340

7 g Carbohydrate
15 g Protein
28 g Fat

Sophia Perez's Burgers with a Difference

These come from health-conscious Sky Blue Soccer School Goalkeeper and Mexico National Team player Sophia Perez. Sophia makes heavy use of vegetables in all of her meals, this being one of her creative ways to do so. She makes these on the grill.

1 pound (450 g) ground turkey
2 cups (50 to 150 g) raw vegetables, including mushrooms, spinach, tomatoes, bell peppers (red, yellow or green)
1 egg

Optional:
For a Mexican flair, add lemon or lime juice, onion and a jalapeno pepper.
For a Chinese flair, use soy sauce, and/or garlic powder.

1. Blend the vegetables in a food processor or blender, until they make a thick paste. You should have about a third the amount of paste as meat.

2. Combine the vegetable paste with the meat and egg. Shape into four half-inch thick patties.

3. Cook in a pre-heated skillet treated with cooking spray or a little oil.

4. Alternatively, wrap and freeze the patties. To prepare them straight from the freezer, cook on a low-heat for about 15 minutes until done.

Yield: 3 servings
Total Calories: 750
Calories per serving: 250

7 g Carbohydrate
26 g Protein
13 g Fat

Tasha Kai's Favorite Fried Rice

Sky Blue FC Forward Tasha Kai's dad says this is Tasha's favorite dish when she comes home to Hawaii for a visit. "I only cook this for get-togethers or a party," he reports. Tasha raves about her dad's cooking. While this is not traditional Hawaiian food, he says, his recipes are "Island flavored dishes." They combine the Kai's family background, which for Tasha means she is a mixture of nine bloods (cultures).

Tasha's dad makes this fried rice with Charsiu (pork), Portuguese sausage, fish cake (available in the oriental section of many supermarkets), and a can of light Spam. We've adapted the recipe to include the more commonly available (vegetarian) sausage and any mild white fish (e.g. haddock, sole). You can easily add more vegetables, such as steamed asparagus, to ramp up the vegetable content.

$1^1/_2$ cups (300 g) uncooked rice
4 tablespoons (60 g) olive oil
5 eggs
1 medium sweet onion, preferably Vidalia, finely diced
$^1/_2$ bunch green onion tops, finely chopped until the white parts
1 11-ounce (310 g) can corn
Garlic powder, pepper and oyster sauce, to taste
Choice of meats, vegetarian sausage, fish

1. Cook rice according to the directions on the package.
2. While the rice is cooking, dice the onion and green onion tops.
3. In a hot wok or large pan, heat 1 tablespoon of olive oil. Scramble the eggs and cook until nearly done. Remove from the heat and put them in large bowl.
4. Wipe the wok clean, add another tablespoon of oil. When heated, add the onion (and meats); cook until done. Add the corn; cook until heated and then add the onion-meat-corn mixture to the bowl with the eggs.
5. Wipe the wok clean, heat another two tablespoons of oil. Add the rice and then the egg-meat mixture. Mix in garlic powder, pepper and oyster sauce. Mix well and enjoy!

Yield: 5 servings   55 g Carbohydrate
Total Calories: 2,000 calories   5 g Protein
Calories per serving: 400   17 g Fat

Aya Miyama's Japanese-style Hamburgers

Aya Miyama, Midfielder on the Los Angeles Sol, offers this twist on the typical American favorite. The biggest difference between a Japanese-style hamburger and an American one is that there is no bun! Tonkastu is typical Japanese sauce which can be purchased at Asian specialty stores, but if you can't find it, use a steak sauce you can sweeten with a small amount of ketchup and add a bit of lemon. Or, you can simply use Worcestershire sauce.

2 pounds (900 g) ground beef, extra lean
1 small onion, chopped
1 tablespoon (15 g) oil, preferably olive or canola
1/4 cup (30 g) bread crumbs, preferably Panko (Japanese bread crumbs, which are widely available in major supermarkets or Asian specialty stores).
3 tablespoons (45 ml) milk
1 egg
1 teaspoon (5 g) salt
1/4 teaspoon (1 g) allspice
Dash of ground pepper

Sauce:
1/4 cup (70 g) ketchup
1/4 cup (60 ml) Tonkatsu sauce or Worcestershire sauce
2 tablespoons (30 ml) cooking wine or sake

Optional: daikon (radish) or ponzu (soy sauce vinegar).

1. Sauté the chopped onion in a small pan with oil; let it cool.
2. In a large bowl, moisten the bread crumbs with milk. Add the rest of the ingredients and mix well.
3. Divide into 8, form into flat oval shapes, and then slightly push down the middle part.
4. Place on heated iron skillet on low setting. Cook until done (approx 5-6 minutes for the first side and about 2-3 minutes for the other side).
5. To make a sauce using the drippings in the skillet, add the ketchup, Tonkatsu or Worcestershire sauce, and cooking wine (or sake). Stir well and cook for a few minutes to let the alcohol evaporate.
6. Optional: Garnish with grated daikon and add a touch of ponzu.

Yield: 8 burgers
Total Calories: 2,200
Calories per serving: 275

7 g Carbohydrate
26 g Protein
16 g Fat

199

Philadelphia Independence Bagel Panini

Philadelphia is famous for its Philly Cheesesteak (thin sliced steak, onions, peppers and melted cheese served on a hoagie roll). This recipe offers a makeover that emphasizes the bread (carbs) over the filling, and cuts back on the fat content of the traditional sandwich.

1 big (4-ounce (120 g)) bagel, preferably whole wheat
1 teaspoon (5 g) olive oil
1 ounce (30 g) sliced low-fat cheese (fresh mozzarella, cheddar, swiss etc.)
3 ounces (120 g) turkey breast or roast beef

Optional: Pesto or mustard for dressing; grilled vegetables (eggplant, zucchini); lettuce and tomato

1. Slice the bagel in half. On the inside of both halves, spread a thin layer of olive oil. Place one half, oil side down, in a pan over medium heat. Place on it the cheese. Place the second half on top, oil side up.
2. Using a heavy weight, or a spatula and "elbow grease," press the bagel flat. When the cooked side is brown and crisp, turn it over and brown the other side. (If you have a panini maker, you can dispense with the "elbow grease.")
3. Remove the bagel from the pan. Open the melted cheese sandwich and put in turkey or roast beef (briefly heat them if you want a completely hot sandwich).
4. Add choice of dressings (mustard, pesto etc.) grilled vegetables or lettuce and tomato.
5. Cut it in half and enjoy.

Yield: 1 hearty sandwich
Total Calories: 550
Calories per serving: 550

60 g Carbohydrate
42 g Protein
16 g Fat

Los Angeles Sol Mexican Pizza

Pizza, a universal soccer favorite, takes on a whole new nutritional level with this colorful three-bean topping! The taste will depend on the strength and flavor of your salsa. If you like a zesty pizza, add more salsa to the pizza before it cooks, or serve extra salsa on the side when it is done.
Alternatively, you can make this pizza with spaghetti or pizza sauce.

2 pounds (900 g) pizza dough, from the supermarket refrigerator/freezer, or a pizza parlor
1 15.5-ounce (440 g) can black beans, drained and rinsed
1 15.5-ounce (440 g) can garbanzo beans, drained and rinsed
1 15.5-ounce (440 g) can kidney beans, drained and rinsed
2 cups (500 g) salsa
2 cups (225 g) grated cheese, such as low-fat cheddar or mozzarella

Optional: Extra salsa

1. Preheat oven to 450° F (230° C). Prepare a large cookie sheet, or two smaller ones, with cooking spray or wipe them with oil.
2. Using your hands or a rolling pin, pull the dough to a size that will fit the large sheet, or divide the dough into two pieces, and make two smaller pizzas. (With the single sheet, you will have thicker crust pizza, but two thin pizzas are easier to make.)
3. Drain and rinse the three cans of beans and combine them in a medium bowl.
4. Distribute a layer of beans on the pizza dough until you have used them all, gently pressing them into the dough so they will stick well.
5. Cover the bean mixture evenly with the salsa, then the grated cheese.
6. Bake for 15 to 20 minutes, until dough is browned on bottom and crisp.

Yield: 8 hefty servings
Total Calories: 4,000
Calories per serving: 500

80 g Carbohydrate
25 g Protein
9 g Fat

Baking Tips

Gloria's teams enjoyed planning "bake-offs" for healthful post-game recovery treats. The players absolutely loved them! To enhance the nutritional value of your home-baked goods, try some of the following:

- Replace up to half of the white flour with whole wheat (whole wheat pastry flour is particularly light).

- Add up to half a cup (60 g) of ground flax seeds, wheat germ or other healthful additions to your recipes.

- Create oat flour by grinding raw rolled oats in the blender or food processor. Replace part of the white flour with this oat flour. In some recipes, such as biscotti or other dense cookies, it actually improves the consistency and the flavor (as well as nutritional content).

- Replace up to half of the oil with applesauce or prune butter.

- Focus on fruit- or vegetable-based baked goods (e.g. raisin cookies; banana, apple, pumpkin or zucchini breads).

Abby Wambach's Date Bars

Washington Freedom Forward Abby Wambach clearly enjoys good food. When Women's Professional Soccer players were asked to list their favorite stores, most chose clothing outlets. Abby's were Whole Foods and Trader Joe's. Below is an easy dessert, perfect for carbo-loading.

$1/_4$ cup (120 g) butter or soft tub margarine
10 ounces (280 g) chopped dates
$1/_2$ to 1 cup (100 to 200 g) sugar
2 eggs
$1/_2$ teaspoon (2 g) salt
$1/_2$ teaspoon (2 g) cinnamon
$1/_4$ teaspoon (1 g) baking powder
$1/_2$ cup (60 g) flour, preferably half whole wheat

Optional: 1 cup (140 g) chopped walnuts

1. Preheat oven to 350° F (180° C).
2. In a medium-sized microwavable bowl, melt the butter or margarine.
3. Add the dates, sugar, eggs, salt and cinnamon. Beat well.
4. Mix the baking powder into the flour and then gently stir that into the date mixture. (Add the nuts.)
5. Pour into an oiled 9" x 9" pan. Bake for 45 minutes, or until a toothpick inserted near the center comes out clean.

Yield: 9 servings
Total Calories: 2,000
Calories per serving: 220

40 g Carbohydrate
2 g Protein
6 g Fat

Allison Falk's Black Bottom Cupcakes

While these are more calorie-dense than nutrient dense, they can be balanced into an overall wholesome sports diet. Says Allison, Defender of the Philadelphia Independence: "Growing up, I knew I could count on my mom to make my favorite black bottom cupcakes for after our important league and tournament games. I always looked forward to eating them in celebration of our team's win!"

1 box (517 g) of dark chocolate cake mix

For the filling:
8 ounces (240 g) cream cheese, softened
1 egg
Dash of salt
$1/3$ cup (70 g) sugar
6 to 8 ounces (170 to 225 g) chocolate chips

1. Preheat oven to 350° F (180° C). Prepare cake batter according to the directions on the box.
2. In a small bowl, beat the cream cheese. Add the egg, salt, sugar. Mix well. Stir in chocolate chips.
3. Spoon the cake batter into muffin tins (use paper liners, coat them with cooking spray for best results) until two-thirds full.
4. Add a heaping tablespoon of the cream cheese mixture on top of each cupcake.
5. Bake for 18 to 21 minutes (or according to package instructions).

Yield: 24 cupcakes
Total Calories: 2,450
Calories per serving: 190

26 g Carbohydrate
3 g Protein
8 g Fat

Washington Freedom Peanut Butter Cereal Bars

This bar has long been a favorite of players of all ages and abilities. Youth teams enthusiastically devour them pre- or post-game as a healthier alternative to cookies. Although almost half the calories are from fat, that fat is from heart-healthy unsaturated fats in the peanut butter and sunflower seeds.

If you use pre-sweetened cereal, cut back on the amount of raisins and skip the chocolate chips entirely. Otherwise, the bars will be overly-sweet.

6 cups (180 to 300 g) of crunchy cereal, such as toasted rice, oat O's or squares, bran buds, etc.
(Mix and match cereals to taste.)
$1^1/_2$ cups (220 g) raisins
$^1/_2$ cup (70 g) sunflower or pumpkin seeds or other nuts
1 cup (170 g) honey
1 16-ounce (450 g) jar natural peanut butter, smooth or chunky
1 teaspoon (5 g) vanilla
$^1/_2$ teaspoon (1 g) cinnamon

Optional: 1 cup (170 g) chocolate chips

1. Combine cereal, raisins, and seeds or nuts in a large bowl.
2. Combine honey and peanut better in a microwavable bowl or saucepan. Heat until well blended. Let cool a bit. Add vanilla and cinnamon.
3. Pour the peanut butter mixture over the cereal mixture; mix well.
4. Press mixture into greased 12" x 16" inch baking pan (a larger pan will make flatter bars).
5. When cool cut into desired-sized squares.

Yield: Makes 5 dozen $1^1/_2$ inch bars
Total Calories: 6,000 (when made from Cheerios)
Calories per serving: 100

12 g Carbohydrate
2 g Protein
5 g Fat

SWEETS AND TREATS

Women's Professional Soccer Apple Snack Cake

This easy-to-carry-and-serve cake is a welcome treat for post-game refueling. Win or lose, teams have always enjoyed this cake and this tradition. It celebrates what Women's Professional Soccer stands for: love of the game!

The original recipe called for 1 cup of oil, but that results in a cake that gets half the calories from fat. We replaced half of the oil with applesauce for an equally tasty cake that does a better job of refueling glycogen-depleted muscles.

---

4 to 5 large cooking apples, such as Macintosh, Macoun, Granny Smith
$1/_4$ cup (50 g) sugar
1 to 2 tablespoons (7 to 14 g) cinnamon
$1/_4$ cup (60 ml) orange juice
4 eggs
1 cup (200 g) sugar
$1/_2$ cup (110 g) oil
$1/_2$ cup (125 g) applesauce, preferably unsweetened
$1/_2$ cup (120 ml) milk
2 teaspoons (10 ml) vanilla extract
$1^1/_2$ teaspoons (7 g) salt
1 tablespoon (15 g) baking powder
3 cups (375 g) flour, preferably half whole wheat (whole wheat pastry flour works best)

---

1. Peel and thinly slice the apples. Place in a large bowl. Sprinkle with 1/4 cup sugar, cinnamon and orange juice. Set aside.

2. In a separate bowl, beat together the eggs, 1 cup sugar, applesauce and oil. Add the milk, vanilla extract and salt.

3. In a small bowl, mix the baking powder into the flours, and add to the egg mixture. Stir until just blended.

4. Oil and flour a 9" x 13", or similar size, pan. Pour in 1/3 of the cake batter, then layer it with half the apples. Put another layer of batter, the rest of the apples, and finish with the last third of the batter. Pour the remaining juice mixture from the apples over the top of the cake. (Batter layers will be very thin. Don't worry if they don't cover all of the apples, since the batter expands during baking.)

5. Bake at 350° F (180° C) for about 40 to 50 minutes, or until a toothpick inserted near the center comes out clean.

Yield: 16 servings
Total Calories: 4,200
Calories per serving: 260

42 g Carbohydrate
5 g Protein
8 g Fat

Acknowledgements:

Sky Blueberry FC Baked French Toast
Adapted from soccer aunt Jennifer Erickson
Black Bean Spinach Dip
Adapted/provided from Jay Will/Eveland soccer families
Peanut Butter Cereal Bars
Adapted from soccer mom Sandy Millstead and Smucker's
Atlanta Beat Tomato Casserole
Adapted from soccer mom Lili Brown

Additional Resources

To find a local sports nutritionist contact:
American Dietetic Association
Tel.: (800) 366-1655
www.eatright.org (click on Find a Nutrition Expert)

Sports Nutrition Dietary Practice Group of the American Dietetic Association
www.SCANdpg.org (use the referral network)

Newsletters
Tufts University Health & Nutrition Letter
Tel.: (800) 274-7581
http://healthletter.tufts.edu

University of California at Berkeley Wellness Letter
Tel.: (386) 447-6328
www.berkeleywellness.com

Catalogs for Nutrition Books and Other Resources:

Nutrition topics:
Nutrition Counseling and Education Services
Tel.: (888) 545-5653
www.ncescatalog.com

Eating disorders:
Gurze Books
Tel.: (800) 756-7533
www.gurze.net

Fitness and sports nutrition:
Human Kinetics
Tel.: (800) 747-4457
www.humankinetics.com

Recommended Reading

Benardot, Dan. *Advanced Sports Nutrition.* Human Kinetics, 2006

Clark, Nancy. *Nancy Clark's Sports Nutrition Guidebook, Fourth Edition.* Human Kinetics, 2008

Colberg, Sheri. *The Diabetic Athlete's Handbook.* Human Kinetics, 2008

Duyff, Roberta. *The American Dietetic Association's Complete Food and Nutrition Guide.* Chronimed Publishing, 2006

Larsen-Meyer, Enette. *Vegetarian Sports Nutrition.* Human Kinetics, 2006

LoBue, Andrea and Marsea Marcus. *The Don't Diet, Live-It! Workbook: Healing Food, Weight & Body Issues.* Gurze Books, 1999

Satter, Ellyn. *Secrets of Feeding a Healthy Family.* Kelcy Press, 1999

Satter, Ellyn. *Your Overweight Child: Helping Without Harming*, Kelcy Press 2005

Soccer Books by Gloria Averbuch
Averbuch, Gloria and Ashley Michael Hammond. *Goal! The Ultimate Guide for Soccer Moms and Dads.* Rodale, 1999

Dorrance, Anson and Gloria Averbuch. *The Vision of a Champion: Advice And Inspiration From The World's Most Successful Women's Soccer Coach.* Huron River Press, fifth printing, 2005

Chastain, Brandi with Gloria Averbuch. *It's Not About the Bra: Play Hard, Play Fair, and Put the Fun Back into Competitive Sports.* HarperCollins, 2004

Averbuch, Gloria, illustrations by Yaakov Guterman. *A Turn for Lucas.* Mitten Press, 2006

For coaches and professionals:

Dunford, Marie Ed. *Sports Nutrition: A Guide for the Professional Working with Active People, Fourth Edition.* American Dietetic Association, 2005

Internet Resources

Sports and Sports Nutrition:

Australian Institute of Sport
www.ais.org.au/nutrition
Comprehensive information on physical fitness and nutrition

Gatorade Sports Science Institute
www.gssiweb.com
Information on endurance sports nutrition

Nancy Clark, MS, RD
www.nancyclarkrd.com
Links to nutrition articles and other nutrition sources; information on teaching materials

Health and Nutrition:

ConsumerLab.com
www.consumerlab.com
Independently tests nutritional supplements and posts the results.

International Food Information Council Foundation
www.foodinsight.org
Geared mostly to health professionals, the site features information on food safety and nutrition

National Library of Medicine, U.S. Department of Health and Human Services
www.nlm.nih.gov
Access to medical journals

Eating disorders:

National Eating Disorders Association
www.NationalEatingDisorders.org
Information, resources, and links for eating disorders

Something Fishy Website on Eating Disorders
www.something-fishy.org
Offers extensive resources and referrals for eating disorders

SOCCER

Women's Professional Soccer
1000 Brannan St., Suite 401
San Francisco, CA 94103
(415) 553-4460
www.womensprosoccer.com

The mission of Women's Professional Soccer (WPS) is to be the premier women's soccer league in the world, and the global standard by which women's professional sports are measured. The teams as of the 2010 season are the Boston Breakers, Chicago Red Stars, FC Gold Pride (Bay Area), Los Angeles Sol, Sky Blue FC (NJ/NY), Saint Louis Athletica, Washington Freedom, Philadelphia Independence and The Atlanta Beat.

American Youth Soccer Organization
12501 S. Isis Ave., Hawthorne, CA 90250
(800) 872-2976
www.ayso.org

Provides soccer development and instruction for children between the ages of 4 and 19 in all 50 states and provides programs for instruction of coaches and referees and child protection education to AYSO volunteers.

National Soccer Coaches Association of America
800 Ann Ave., Kansas City, KS 66101
(800) 458-0678
www.nscaa.com

Based in Kansas City, Kan., the NSCAA is the largest coaches' organization in the United States, and fulfills its mission of coaching education through a nationwide program of clinics and week-long courses, teaching more than 4,000 soccer coaches each year.

U.S. Adult Soccer Association National Headquarters
9152 Kent Avenue, Suite C-50, Lawrence, IN 46216
(317) 541-8564
www.usasa.com

The national organization for amateur soccer in the United States; it represents the fifth tier in the American Soccer Pyramid and purports to have over 250,000 adult members playing within its leagues and teams, making it the country's largest division of organized soccer at the adult levels.

United States Club Soccer
716 8th Ave. N., Myrtle Beach, S.C. 29577
(843) 429-0006
www.usclubsoccer.org

US Club Soccer is a non-profit organization committed to the support and development of competitive soccer clubs. It is founded on the belief that soccer clubs, which are in the business of elite player development, need an organization of their own to foster growth, address concerns, and sanction and provide programs with a minimum of rules and restrictions.

US Youth Soccer Association
9220 World Cup Way, Frisco, TX 75034
(800)-4-SOCCER
www.usyouthsoccer.org

USYSA is the youth affiliate and largest member of the United States Soccer Federation (ussoccer.com), the governing body for soccer in the United States. US Youth Soccer includes fifty-five state youth soccer associations, one per state except for California, New York, Ohio, Pennsylvania and Texas, which each have two state associations. Over 3,000,000 youth players between ages 5-19 are registered with USYSA.

Index

Photo Credits

Photo editor: Robyn McNeil
Cover design: Sabine Groten
Cover photos: Cori Alexander; © r3bel/Fotolia.com
Section photos: Cori Alexander
Inside photos: p. 12: John Todd/WPS
p. 21, 29, 85, 161: Cori Alexander
p. 100: David Durochik/Chicago Red Stars
p. 180: Terry Geerdts/A Pretty Pixel
All other photos by Robyn McNeil